Radical Vessels

A cry to the 21st century church

By

Dale Haight

Copyright © 2005 by Dale Haight

Radical Vessels
by Dale Haight

Printed in the United States of America

ISBN 1-59781-314-1

All rights reserved solely by the author. The author guarantees all contents are original and do not infringe upon the legal rights of any other person or work. No part of this book may be reproduced in any form without the permission of the author. The views expressed in this book are not necessarily those of the publisher.

Unless otherwise noted all Scripture quotations are from the New American Standard Bible – updated version ©1960, 1962, 1963, 1968, 1971, 1972, 1973, 1977, 1995 by the Lockman Foundation. Used by permission.

Scriptures taken from the New International Version are noted as NIV. ©1973, 1978 and 1984 by International Bible Society. Used by permission of Zondervan. All rights reserved.

Scriptures noted as NKJV are from the Holy Bible – New Kings James Version ©1982 by Thomas Nelson, Inc.

www.xulonpress.com

Table of Contents

Dedication		vii
Endorsements		ix
Foreword		xi
Preface		xiii

Part 1	*The call To a 21st Century Church*	*19*
Chapter 1	The call to arms	21
Chapter 2	The call to pray	27
Chapter 3	The cost of freedom	33
Chapter 4	The commission	37

Part 2	*Becoming Vessels*	*41*
Chapter 5	Vessels of honor	43
Chapter 6	Vessels of revival	49
Chapter 7	Vessels of purity	55
Chapter 8	Vessels of preparation	59
Chapter 9	Vessels of restoration	65
Chapter 10	Vessels of favor	71
Chapter 11	Vessels of the presence	75
Chapter 12	Vessels of purpose	79
Chapter 13	Vessels of completion	87
Chapter 14	Vessels of hunger	93

Part 3	***Being Vessels***	***101***
Chapter 15	The "In-Between Place"	103
Chapter 16	The "Go Group"	111
Chapter 17	Getting there from here	119
Chapter 18	Some 21st Century Radical Vessels	123
Epilogue		131

Dedication

Proverbs 31 speaks of a virtuous woman. I am married to such a woman. I dedicate this book to one of the most radical vessels I know, my wife Trudy. You are a constant reminder to me that pursuing the Lord must be the passion of my life. You have raised our family to know that God is near and that there is no place like home. I am so blessed to walk with you in this life.

Endorsements

"This book is written to breathe renewed spiritual vitality into the life of the believer and the corporate life of the church. I commend this book to you, not simply because Dale is a valued and trusted friend, but because his many years of impactful pastoral ministry have given him the perspective and qualifications to address the issues in this book. Conversational in style, Dale's casual approach will sneak up on you and read your mail. May the Lord use this impassioned call to ignite your spiritual walk with fresh fire!"
—Bob Sorge, author of Exploring Worship and
The Fire of Delayed Answers. (www.oasishouse.net)

"Webster's Dictionary definition of the word radical is 'extreme'. In a sense the word radical has a negative connotation. Perhaps that's why so many Christians shy away from being extreme or radical. What do you think? Wouldn't you say that Jesus' life, the cross and the resurrection was a bit extreme, perhaps even radical? As a matter of fact, Jesus Himself was radical. The opposite of being radical would be mediocre. William Somerset Maugham made this statement: 'Only a mediocre man is always at his best.' The sad thing is that so many Christians are always at their 'best'. I have just finished reading Radical Vessels and realize the necessity for every believer to read this book. For some who are experiencing

the posture of a radical vessel it will be an encouragement to embrace new challenges that bring you to an even more radical identity in Him. For others who are just beginning to embrace their Christian walk with an extreme attitude, with Dale's leading, this journey points to a higher calling with the guarantee that God has provided all that we need to become radical vessels. Dale says in this book, 'There is no room for quitting in the midst of waiting.' We are aiming for completion and must keep our aim true. As you read Radical Vessels take aim!"

—Don Richter, President and director of Harvest Preparation International Ministries, Sarasota, Florida (www.harvestpreparation.com)

"Dale has tuned into the voice of the Holy Spirit with refreshing clarity and accuracy. His words provoke us to fix our position in this world based upon spiritual coordinates and clear signals from the throne of God."

—Dale Fife, from the Foreword

Foreword
Radical Vessels

Several years ago I was introduced to the groundbreaking technology of the Global Positioning System (GPS). It was just beginning to impact the culture and would quickly revolutionize the way we navigate and communicate in the twenty first century. One of our church members invited me to the parking lot behind our church building and removed a handheld device from his suit coat pocket. "Pastor, you have got to see this," he said, with the excitement of a child playing with a new toy.

I watched in amazement as he pushed the buttons and explained the process taking place. "This instrument is now locating satellites in orbit around the earth. Once it has logged on to three different satellites, they will triangulate our position on earth and our exact location here in this parking lot will be flashed onto the screen. It is so accurate that it will even give us our altitude above sea level and the precise spot where we are standing within a few feet."

I found myself reliving that experience as I read Dale Haight's book, *Radical Vessels*. Dale has tuned into the voice of the Holy Spirit with refreshing clarity and accuracy. His words provoke us to fix our position in this world based upon spiritual coordinates and clear signals from the throne of God. His insight not only identifies our location as the body of Christ, but also issues a clear summons to fulfill the mandate our Lord has issued. We are to be in the world, but not of it. We are to resist the pressures of culture that want to squeeze us into its mold. Instead, we are called to transform society as light and salt in the world. In other words, we are to be 'radical vessels'.

Dale encourages us to reconnect with our bona-fide historical and spiritual roots. Each chapter whets the spiritual appetite to go deeper, to press further, to step past the restraints of religion and culture, into the God dimension of spiritual power, reality and relationship. I am convinced of his accuracy, because I know his authenticity. He speaks and writes from a heart of worship and intimacy with God. His love of the scriptures, and gratitude for the church are refreshing. His enthusiasm for all things 'God breathed' is exemplary. He walks with a spiritual limp that conveys strength in humility.

Dale is a colleague, brother, and friend. We have traveled together on the mission field and I have had the joy and privilege of ministering at Praise! Fellowship where he and Trudy are the founding pastors. I thank God for these two 'radical vessels', the message that God is pouring through them into the church, and the good fruit of their labor.

Radical Vessels is not a criticism. It is a critique. It calls us to the place of surrender to the Master Potter, so that we can become more effective in His service. The fields are white unto harvest. Dale's heart cry echoes my own: "God, send more laborers."

Dr. Dale A Fife, President,
Mountain Top Global Ministries,
Founding Pastor, The Potter's House,
Farmington, Connecticut
Author; The Secret Place,
Passionately Pursuing God's Presence
The Hidden Kingdom,
Journey Into the Heart of God

Preface

I wish to invite you to take a journey. For far too many Christians the road of Christian experience has taken a toll that wearies the heart and wears out the body and mind. It ought not to be so! As I wrote this book I asked myself if this was simply a need to write in order to get my heart down on paper or could the church really use this information, already having a plethora of books on a variety of subjects? Could the body of Christ really need a book that addresses some strong contemporary concerns, exploring some rather untouchable areas and find purpose in a life filled with so many questions and seemingly few answers?

As I began compiling this book a few years ago and intensified my work in the past few months it occurred to me that the church is in real need of revival. Although we have just come through some major times of refreshing it seemed as though it was time to prepare for what I call "the next of God". If the Lord is up to something fresh and new and if there is an outpouring coming, as many of us believe, how will we be partakers? How will we come into the fresh thing and not miss the opportunity that is presented whenever God is on the move? We have to look back in order to look ahead and embrace the new thing. We must learn from our history and make plans for the future. But this is not a book about examining the past failures and attempting to correct things as much as it is about a challenge about becoming something that most Spirit-filled

Christians long to become. With the intensity of new passionate worship and a revival of sorts for a love of the Word of God, my purpose is to challenge us to come to an alignment with the Lord's purposes for the individual and the church.

I am a pastor/teacher. When the Lord called me to the pastoral ministry at 21 years of age I had absolutely no idea what that meant! My perspective as a pastor has allowed me a bit of objectivity as I have watched good people who were in love with Jesus struggle to find purpose in life, what their "ministry" is and the fortitude to survive the constant and rather efficient attacks of an enemy bent on our destruction.

I saw many around me simply come to the place of giving up and becoming content to just "go with the flow", whatever that meant. While they loved Jesus they had lost their passion for Him. While they attended church meetings they were not concerned any longer about becoming the church.

I have seen the unhealthy and wearying competition between churches and members as they have jockeyed for position and respect. I have seen pastors and leaders who once carried fire that burned brightly, begin to settle and grow tired. I have seen other leaders, who when they were in their prime were a formidable force for the kingdom, come to the place of resignation, burnout, and failure.

I have also felt myself slipping into a place of desperation. I came to a place of wondering if this whole thing was even real or had we just made it all up? This "dark night of the soul" caused me to slip into a state that I never had thought I would come to. I had not lost my faith…I still loved Jesus…but the discouragement of things around me was taking its toll. My lack of passion for Jesus and especially for the lost began to really scare me. I would look at the obituaries in the newspaper and unlike times in the early part of my ministry, I no longer had real concern about the eternity of those who had slipped from this life to the next.

Passionless, hurting and feeling a sense of defeat, I began to cry out to God. Praise the Lord He heard my cry! He then began to bring people into my life that inspired me. It was the seasoned leaders and ministers that impacted me most. These servants had, as they say, been there and done that. Many had devastating experiences in their journey that God had used to form their destiny in Him. All of them had some things in common. They knew the Lord better today then they had known Him before their wilderness experiences. They worshipped Him more passionately then they ever had before. Each one had defining moments that brought them to intimacy in Christ that I longed for. They had become *Radical Vessels* in and for the kingdom. They found that the time spent on their faces before the Lord could not be replaced with anything or anyone else.

The things I learned from this journey and from the great *personnel files* of the Word of God are revealed in this book. It is a compassionate plea to the church to become something more than a ritual filled, committee conscious non-entity in the earth and be transformed into the army that God has intended it to be.

We are living in an interesting time for the church. There is a constant pulling going on as men and women of faith attempt to discover what it truly means to be "the church". While some advocate for the concept that "house churches" and various movements is the New Testament normative, others, like me, believe that there are hidden truths that can only be discovered when we look at the larger picture.

Rather than bring confusion I will attempt to instruct in clarity that the church is really about the people of God finding their place in His kingdom. It includes meeting and breaking bread from house to house, while at the same time gathering the congregation for times of worship, instruction and fellowship in ways that only the larger gathering of the body provides and is totally biblical. As the members of the body of Christ discover that God has called each one to a vital purpose in the earth we become useful for the Master. Unless and until we find our place as a vessel we will simply remain a motionless pile of clay lumped up in the corner. We are called to be extreme in faith, witness and function. We are summoned to the Potter's wheel for formation and preparation. As we are molded into the people of God's own choosing we are liberated to become *Radical Vessels!*

I wish to thank some people who have shaped my life significantly. I am grateful to God for their input, suggestions and mentoring in my life before the Lord and in this work in particular. Bob Sorge, Dr. Dale Fife, Pastor Randy Stewart, and Dr. Michael L. Brown have been strong influences in my life and are powerful and gifted teachers. I want to especially acknowledge Pastor Don Richter, the president and founder of Harvest Preparation International Ministries, Sarasota, Florida, for his fatherhood in my spiritual journey. Don opened my life to the nations and as a result I am profoundly and eternally grateful.

I am particularly thankful to and for my wife Trudy. She is the greatest gift from God and is constantly challenging me to be a greater vessel for God, as we walk this life together and pastor the passionate people of Praise! Fellowship of Russell, PA. Together we praise God for our children and grandchildren. Our quiver is full! I am also grateful to Trudy for her faithful and tireless work in helping to edit and proof the manuscript for this book.

I wish to thank the staff at Xulon Press for their vision to give opportunity and occasion for Christian authors to have a pipeline through which to communicate powerful and vital truths to the nations.

Thanks to our staff pastors at Praise! Fellowship, Rick and Sandie Rohlin, Bill and Nila Schneider and John and Maryanne Agricola and everyone who attends the fellowship, as we are all together challenged to become *Radical Vessels!*

There are some individuals that have spoken clearly into my life. Some of them are dear friends that I have walked with and others more casual acquaintances, but all have been instrumental in the formation of the things contained in this book. I am grateful for Jim W. Goll, whom I met and had a season of days with in Nashville a number of years ago, as ten men gathered in a little room to seek the face of the Lord and to hear His voice. Jim's prophetic voice into my life remains to this day a confirmation of the grace of God and call of the Lord in my life. I thank the Lord for my dear friends Chris and Carole Beatty, Gerrit Gustafson, Chip Richter, Dr. Fount Shults, Ronnie Harjo and Randy Rothwell. I am thankful for the ministry imparted to me through Bob Mumford,

Bernard Evans, Jim Erb, Marty Nystrom, Pastor Ray Forstrom and the late Father Ed Shower and many others whose teaching and ministry has touched me and matured me in the Lord.

I have the privilege of being a part of two pastors' prayer groups that meet each week and seek the Lord for revival. My dear friends, God is at work and we must continue to meet, even more as we see the day of the Lord approaching. I thank God for you.

Most of all I give thanks to Jesus Christ. He saved my life and gave me peace for He is peace. He is the most radical of all vessels who have ever walked this planet. I look forward to seeing Him face to face!

—DEH

Part One

The Call to a 21st Century Church

CHAPTER 1

The Call to Arms

"...For to one is given the word of wisdom through the Spirit, to another, the word of knowledge through the same Spirit, to another faith by the same Spirit, to another the gifts of healings by the same Spirit..." 1 Corinthians 12:8-9

God is so good! He gives beyond our thinking and makes a way where there appears to be none. He makes a provision when all seems lost and without hope.

The Church is in a strange state today. Regardless of where you go in the world, there is a sense that not all that can be done is being done. There are glimmers of hope and excitement. I read recently that there are more than 100,000 coming to Jesus daily in the world. Certainly this is reason to celebrate. Yet as I speak to leaders most everywhere, there is a sense of not quite making it. Churches are closing at an alarming rate in North America. There is despair in much of the world. Economies are suffering and many nations are struggling in so many ways. It seems that it would be a good time for the Lord to intervene and make Himself known.

God has always chosen to use people. He created the earth and then mankind to rule over the earth. What makes us think that He will simply usher in a reign of peace, joy and revival without the participation of mankind? The Lord God has established a pattern and the church is required to walk and work within that framework. True revival can and will come provided the church finally gets its role figured out.

Problem #1 *We think we are in the move of God!*

One major problem that we now face is that the Body of Christ has, in many ways, begun to think that we have finally made it. Many churches grow numerically or have a series of meetings where the glory of the Lord is brushed up against and we think that we have arrived. We canvass our areas with ads for our local assembly and a few people show up unexpectedly and we declare "revival". Our folly then continues as we run competition with one another gaining "new" members; although, it is simply transfer membership (I choose to not call it growth) we are touted as the major work of our region...and we believe it!

We are NOT in revival. In fact, as Dr. Michael L. Brown has stated, we may not even recognize revival when it does come. As he has said numerous times, "We don't know what we don't know!" When God comes do we not expect that something major will accompany His coming? Historically, revival periods or awakenings have been marked by two major events in the church: 1) true repentance on the part of believers for their worldliness and 2) a hunger for the Lord accompanied by a burden for the lost. They have also come during times of great desperation and trouble.

Revival has also affected the world around the church. When true awakening begins there may only be a casual interest in what is happening. The secular society will take note of a church that is experiencing rapid growth, for example. They will begin to make statements such as, "What a great thing must be going on 'out there'", or "You must be doing something right!" These statements can be used to address the curiosity that a worldly person may be having about the question as to why people are going to church to begin with. However, as true revival begins to take root a church will begin to carry a burden for the lost. When this happens, they will seek the Lord regarding how to win the lost or reach out to their city or community. The fellowship then begins to apply what the Lord is revealing. Usually the result of outreach does not at first meet with receptivity among the onlookers. In fact, they may become at least mildly offended by this "church trying to get me." However, as the Holy Spirit begins to use the believers to make an impact on the area something interesting will begin to take place. Perhaps significant individuals begin to attend meetings and some may even get saved. When word gets out that influential government leaders are becoming Christians or that some hopelessly lost addicts are being set free from their addiction as they surrender to Jesus Christ, a true revival spirit will invade a community.

Problem #2 Some Christians are not particularly fond of growth!

One very interesting phenomenon that I have personally witnessed is the sense among some otherwise "on fire" Christians that big is too big! Statements begin to ring out from the midst of the people, "I don't know anyone here anymore" or "We used to have much closer fellowship here" and words of this nature. The problem is that we do not have a kingdom of God mentality. If you want to see the critical spirit let loose on a congregation all you need to have is a bit of true revival. It appears to me that the real culprit is our *need to control* things. People, especially those who have been at the very beginning of a church plant or at the start of a season of revival, seem to struggle to one degree or another with numbers. These attitudes and actions taken as a result, whether by members or their leaders, will most certainly curtail revival. Leaders must be sure that they have pure motives when it comes to growing. Members must be willing to have God do His work in their camp, releasing the outcome to the Lord of the harvest.

We are called to arms. We are fighting a battle against the powers of darkness that are trying to keep people out of heaven. We are taking an offensive position against the devil himself and we must take this battle seriously. Every member of Christ's body is vital (see 1 Corinthians 12:14). We cannot back down as the Lord begins adding daily to the numbers of those being saved. As God

gives the church strategies to see revival in our time, we must be willing to lay down our plans and go with God's. God's will is that His church must expand. Jesus paid the ultimate price that this could happen. When we decide that "small" is better that "big", based simply on our preferences, we are not in a move of God any longer but are rather in a move of our own.
Please allow me to take just a paragraph to address what I perceive to be the problems concerning "transfer growth" as some call it.

Let me first tell you that I am going to be very candid. You may want to put this book down after reading this statement, but I hope that you will hear me out. *Not all transfer is bad!* Let us face it; some churches have outlived their purpose or have died long ago and deserve a better death than we are willing to give them. Dudley Hall once said concerning dead and dying churches, "If it cannot be resurrected let it die. If it dies bury it, lest it begin to stink!" Please do not get me wrong…if there is the possibility that a fellowship can receive revival and be resurrected, let us go for it. But many of our churches have died in their dead traditions, having the form of godliness but denying the power thereof. To be a part of something that is sounding its death knoll is very discouraging. But if God is saying, "enough…this work has had its day and it was a good day…let it enter into its rest" how can we get religious and keep it on life support? Perhaps God is in certain types of transfer membership after all.

I must also point out that if a ministry is fixated on taking others from their call to a particular body they are missing something of great importance. If a local church is not concerned about the salvation of those around them, they are missing the great command of Jesus to reach the lost in their own back yard. I will speak later of some outreach that churches can employ that will spark their church into a new season of kingdom thinking.

We must not fall prey to the notion that people simply shifting around is true growth, but at the same time we must recognize that some need to move on to find truth and personal growth.

Realizing that becoming vessels in the service of Jesus is paramount, personal growth is essential. We are called to arms, being equipped for every good work. 2 Timothy 2:21 says, "…if anyone cleanses himself...he will be a vessel for honor, sanctified and useful for the Master, prepared for every good work." To know revival corporately we must know it personally. To know it personally we must recognize our call to arms and be formed by the Potter for our mission.

Are you prepared to respond to this call to arms? I believe that you want to be. So, read on and open up to all that the Holy Spirit would do to make you a vessel for His use.

CHAPTER 2

The Call to Pray

"Pray without ceasing" 1 Thessalonians 5:17

If there is one thing that continues to be missing in the life of the American church it is prayer. In the land of many prayer conferences, calls to prayer, a national day of prayer, and a constant barrage of books on the theme, there is dryness in the practice of prayer that is without parallel.

Before you get too concerned that this is simply a critical chapter, read on. There are some glimmers of hope surrounding this particular issue and some major changes have been occurring over the past years in our culture. But before I speak to those positives, we must take a look at what appears to be the most visible missing link in our churches.

Attendance at some American churches has realized some levels of numerical growth. Bible believing gatherings are realizing an upshot in attendance that is unprecedented in this generation. At the same time there is a decline in desire for the prayer meeting in many churches. Prayer meetings, it seems, must be clothed with certain gimmicks in order to draw people near. Prayer is a great theme for workshops and conferences across the land. There has been a call issued to pray from many leaders. There have been times when it would seem that we were about to burst into a true prayer revival. After a short while, however, the prayer meetings taper off and those remaining faithful to the powerful issues of this aspect of spiritual warfare dwindle to include those who were committed to this ministry before the conference! Having been accused of too much negativity in this arena, I will now become a bit self-disclosing, if I may.

My personal prayer life is in need of revival! I love the presence of the Lord. Time spent before the Father is precious to me and very difficult to guard with all of the time consuming issues of the pastoral ministry. The need to be available to people and to be involved with virtually every area of the events of the gathering, it is very easy for me to "put off" the season of prayer that I am called to each day. I have set aside time each day to meet with God. From early each and *every* morning to about 10 A.M., I am "scheduled" to be praying. Except that Monday mornings there is the staff pastors' meeting to prepare for; on Tuesdays I teach at our ministry school. Then there is Thursday golf and I think that you can see where I am going with this. Here I am...a pastor with my full-time commitment to God and His work. I have the ability to say "no" to certain things and spend time with the Lord every day, but inevitably have *stuff* that gets in the way of my intention.

I have now found a special "clause" in the Word that gets me out of just praying without having to miss out on these other distractions. "Pray without ceasing", the Bible says. Okay, here we go...I can only pray without ceasing if I am praying all the time. So I will simply maintain "an attitude" of prayer no matter what I am doing, right? The Holy Spirit then reminds me that this is nothing less than a cop out. I somehow have been confused about maintaining a prayerful attitude without taking the time that God requires of my *undivided attention*. Prayer without ceasing is not really about simply having a prayer attitude all the time. While the principle of staying in the presence no matter what I am doing is a good one, there is a time and place where I must come before the throne of grace without fail.

It is in this secret place that I will receive from the Lord the truths that He has for my life. I need this specific direction in order to function. Should I desire to become a *radical vessel* for God, I will need to be so close to Him that I can feel His breath, so to speak.

My wife needs special time with just me. If we pretend that we can do fine in our relationship if we are simply in the same room with each other, in spite of all the distractions and activities around us, we will miss the most important of all that relationship can bring: intimacy. Without intimacy the relationship soon grows lukewarm. Many marriages have ended due to a lack of intimate time being cultivated between the two that have become one. The Lord has given us a picture of His desired relationship with us. It is the analogy of marriage that is to give us the clearest view of our relationship with our Lord (see Ephesians 5:32). However, for many the relationship following the marriage ceremony and subsequent honeymoon has gone cold, or at the least, lukewarm. God says that this is not an acceptable relationship between His bride and Him. In Revelation the Laodicean church has fallen out of love with God just as the Ephesian church had as indicated in Revelation 2. It has become cold and impersonal. It comes home from work each day believing that its spouse will simply understand the busyness of the day and how tired and worn out it is, and simply continues the marriage without correction or counsel. The "faithful and true Witness, the Beginning of the creation of God, says this: 'I know your deeds, that you are neither cold nor hot; I wish that you were cold or hot.'" Revelation 3:14b-15. Deeds or works are very important with respect to evaluation. We can determine where we are by our actions. When we cease to have intimacy with God, when we stop unceasing prayer, we will become tepid in our relationship with the Lord. God hates this for a number of reasons. First, because He longs to have a solid relationship with His creation, God is so in love with our prayer times that He calls us to them.

> " 'You shall give to the Levitical priests who are from the offspring of Zadok, who **draw** near to Me to minister to Me,' declares the Lord GOD" Ezekiel 43:19

> "***Draw** me after you and let us run together! The king has*

brought me into his chambers." "We will rejoice in you and be glad; We will extol your love more than wine. Rightly do they love you." Song of Solomon 1:4

God so desires us to come to Him. He makes a way for us to do so and has a divine expectation that the stated created purpose of man, which is to love the Lord and fellowship with Him, is vital to us.

The second reason is that our fellowship with God is important to us as well! If He is the air that we breathe, as one songwriter puts it, than how can we spend even a moment without Him?

The Purpose of Praying

Prayer has purpose. We are called to pray. It is God's desire to be in fellowship with us. Unless and until we gain this understanding we cannot become a radical vessel for Him.

Today there are many glimmers of hope regarding prayer and intercession. I have the privilege of traveling in the body of Christ rather extensively. Most of my invitations are the result of my teaching on issues of worship. One of the major worship teachings in the past few years has been that of the harp and bowl. This is in reference to Revelation 5:8 *"When He had taken the book, the four living creatures and the twenty-four elders fell down before the Lamb, each one holding a harp and golden bowls full of incense, which are the prayers of the saints."* The concept involves the use of musical worship and intercession (prayer) together in the presence of the Lord as a means most effective. "Harp and Bowl Centers" have been opening all over North America in the past several years. Many churches have developed watch night services and some have begun 24/7 worship and prayer gatherings. In Kansas City the International House of Prayer has been in this type of ministry over the past few years and is a great mentor ministry to others. Perhaps the Lord is getting the attention of His church in this regard. Without question if we get the message that prayer is not only vital but a strategic key to revival in our time we will see something like no one has seen in our lifetimes.

There are other strategic ministries that are in response to God's call upon the church to pray. We are still doing more teaching on prayer than we are applying the principles. However, radical vessels are not interested in ways to avoid the dealings of God. They are busy finding the heart of the Father and pursuing passionately the strategies of the kingdom. *Pray without ceasing!*

CHAPTER 3

The Cost of Freedom

"Act as free men, and do not use your freedom as a covering for evil, but use it as bond slaves of God."
1 Peter 2:16

Freedom is a most powerful word in our culture. In North America we tend to take the concept of freedom for granted. All of us have lived with liberty as a way of life. Although we have been tested in this since September 11, 2001, we continue to know this liberty as no other nation on earth. However, our attitude reflects a type of freedom that may not be free at all! Think of it. We plainly state our "rights" and expect that those rights will be protected forever. Even as 21st century Christians we have a concept that freedom, as we have known it, is the paramount issue of life. Yet, we do not truly have a God-concept of liberty, do we? What we have instead is a cultural concept that we attempt to shape our Christian experience to.

    I have spent most of my Christian experience in ministry and much of that as a worship leader. I have heard more times that you could imagine the phrases that describe our worship experiences. "That was really great worship; it really touched my heart." "Wow! We really 'felt' the presence of the Lord in that worship today." Or conversely, "The pastor must be having a bad day today. I didn't get anything out of that worship time." The problem is that our libertarianism has created a dangerous view of what it means to gather for worship and to be worshippers. Somehow we have determined that worship is more about "us" than about God! Historically, when this has happened it has meant some pretty difficult times for the people of the Lord.

In Exodus 32 Moses had been having a powerfully significant time with the Lord God Almighty, to say the least. *"When the people saw that Moses delayed to come down from the mountain, the people assembled about Aaron and said to him, 'Come, make us a god who will go before us; as for this Moses, the man who brought us up from the land of Egypt, we do not know hat has become of him.'"* When people take worship into their own hands and then decide how that worship should look and feel, they miss God altogether. In verse 33 God pronounces a devastating judgment upon those who had willfully sinned in this act. Although the Lord relented in His initial sentence to destroy all of them, the righteous desire of God brought judgment upon the instigators and they were *"blotted out of My book."* Do not mess with worship. There is no freedom that caters to our own selfish desires. We are liberated to a purpose. This purpose is to be a "covering" for evil. Our freedom is intended to bring about others' freedom. When we miss the truth that we have been freed to become servants of God we miss a most important lesson.

Purchased for God

The price has been paid to set us free from the curse of sin and death. Jesus Christ fulfilled the righteous requirement of God's law and shed His own blood that we could know this liberty. Our freedom has a cost to us as well. We no longer live, but Christ lives in us (see Galatians 2:20).

Knowing that I am free to become all that God has intended is only a beginning. This book is about becoming vessels of the Lord. The implication is that we are set free to become owned by God Himself. We are not our own for we have been purchased with a great price, the blood of Jesus Christ (see 1 Corinthians 6:20). Before we can bring freedom to anyone else, we must become free ourselves. Before we can lead anyone to a life giving and life changing relationship with the Lord we must have that life ourselves. Therefore, it is obvious to me that, while we may want a great and mighty move of the Lord and great freedom all around, we must know in our hearts that we are totally and absolutely good with God. I invite you, before you turn another page, to give your heart to Jesus and do not forget to give the rest of your life to Him as well. Once that is done you are ready to become vessels for Him; *Radical Vessels* for the cause of the Lord.

CHAPTER 4

The Commission

"...called according to His purpose." Romans 8:28

I have always been a bit perplexed by Jesus' statement in Matthew 22:14, *"For many are <u>called</u> but few are <u>chosen</u>."* I know that this is not all that complicated. God has beckoned to many to come and find their hope and salvation in Christ, but only a few respond to this call. Another theology says that this supports the idea that God has predestined those who will be saved and those who will not. I will not take the space to make commentary on an issue that has caused so many to be perplexed. I will, however, spend some time with a fresh concept concerning the issues of being "called" and "chosen". Let us take a careful look at this parable:

Matthew 22

> *"The kingdom of heaven may be compared to a king who gave a wedding feast for his son. And he sent out his slaves to call those who had been invited to the wedding feast, and they were unwilling to come. Again he sent out other slaves saying, 'Tell those who have been invited, "Behold, I have prepared my dinner; my oxen and my fattened livestock are*

all butchered and everything is ready; come to the wedding feast.' But they paid no attention and went their way, one to his own farm, another to his business, and the rest seized his slaves and mistreated them and killed them. But the king was enraged, and he sent his armies and destroyed those murderers and set their city on fire. Then he said to his slaves, 'the wedding is ready, but those who were invited were not worthy. 'Go therefore to the main highways, and as many as you find there, invite to the wedding feast.' Those slaves went out into the streets and gathered together all they found, both evil and good; and the wedding hall was filled with dinner guests. But when the king came in to look over the dinner guests, he saw a man there who was not dressed in wedding clothes, and he said to him, 'Friend, how did you come in here without wedding clothes?' And the man was speechless. Then the king said to the servants, 'Bind him hand and foot, and throw him into the outer darkness; in that place there will be weeping and gnashing of teeth.' For many are called, but few are chosen."

The context of this passage is the parable of a king who gave a wedding feast for his son. Concisely, when those who rejected the invitation had done so the invitation went out to those who, in modern terms, would have felt unworthy, unwanted, and normally uninvited to anything. Interestingly, there was a man who somehow made it to the banquet without having properly prepared to come to it. He was not wearing the wedding clothes that were required. This meant something to the hearers of Jesus. There are three "groups" of people mentioned here. There are those who initially rejected the invitation, there are those who received an unexpected all-expenses paid holiday and there is this one who thought he could do it his own way. I list him as a *group* because he is representative of many people today. Two out of three met rejection to something that was offered freely. I want to take a look at this last guy, the one who lived by the theme of that "great prophet" Frank Sinatra, "I did it my way!"

This man must have received an invitation. While others were preparing to go to the feast this man was likely off doing something that seemed important to him at the time. When it was time to attend to the business of the wedding this man did not have the insight or willingness to honor the son of the king. Instead this invited guest threw on some fairly decent clothes that he thought would pass muster and showed up, even obtaining his seat in the hall. Not long afterward the king made his appearance. Like a proud father the king was no doubt bursting with pleasure at the great plans designed for his son's big day. All of a sudden he looked out and saw something that appeared strange. He noticed that this man was not wearing the normal and accepted attire for such a special occasion. It may even be that the king, not wanting any embarrassment for his son, had provided all the guests with their robes but this man cast the provision aside and did what a rebel often does and thought to himself, "If they can't accept me just the way I am then too bad!" Well, it was too bad...for him. He was cast out of the party, not even to return to his home and family, but thrown into a place familiar to the hearers of Jesus. It was the prison of judgment, where those who had committed only the most vile of crimes were sentence to spend time. In this place there was total rejection that caused much weeping and unrelieved sorrow.

A Higher Calling

The call and commission are clear. God has given each of us an assignment in Him. We obtain the commission from Jesus Christ Himself, Who has paid the price for our liberty and has called us to serve Him without shame or reservation. He has provided all that we need to become radical vessels. We are called to wage a war against the forces of darkness that attempt to convince those receiving the invitation that they do not need "saved". The same evil forces have been defeated by the blood of the Lamb that was slain. God calls us to intimacy (prayer) and gives each one an assignment. When we move into this fullness in Him we are ready to become His vessels...radical vessels for the advancement of His Kingdom.

Part 2

Becoming Vessels

CHAPTER 5

Vessels of Honor

"The Call is Greater than the fall!"

There is a looming question for virtually each and every believer in Christ: "Have I made room for everything God wants to do through and in me?" This question must stay at the forefront of my thinking as a Christian.

Principle #1 - The devil has a plan for your life!

Some people do not like to think about the devil. In fact, many Christians reel at the thought of an opposing being. If we would only talk about God and His goodness and mercy and leave all of that weird satanic stuff out of the church, we would be far better off. But the truth of the matter is that the devil is mentioned so much in the Bible, in one form or other, that to ignore this issue is to sidestep the very thing that keeps most people from the Kingdom and most Kingdom people from their King.

Picture this, if you will...the enemy of your soul calling a regular staff meeting. Present at the meeting are a number of lesser beings called demons. They have met to discuss a major issue of their business...YOU! Together they consort and devise a plan that will cause you, a believer in Christ Jesus, to have doubt about your life, call, walk and future. They begin to talk about your vulnerabilities. They have discovered after watching you for a long while that you are susceptible to getting down on yourself, of having feelings of unworthiness and hopelessness. They conclude their meeting with a resolution draft that some of them will hang out near you (because they cannot any longer get in you) and whisper little things toward you. Here you are, having a great day. The sun is shining and there is not a cloud in the sky. You have just had a great morning of prayer and personal worship with your Savior. All is going well. You get in your car to head to the office or to the mall, when all of a sudden you remember that today you have made a commitment to take your Aunt Mabel to lunch and you really do not like her much! The last time you were together all she wanted to do was criticize you for your faith. She had much gossip to share about your pastor's wife and the view of the neighborhood about your church. But she is your father's sister and the last living relative on that side of the family, so you told her (not *really lying,* just trying to be kind) that you really enjoyed your last outing and look forward to getting together again soon. On your way to town this day you begin recalling the past meeting and then it happens...a small voice begins to speak from the back of the car, "You are such a hypocrite! You have no real love for Mabel. You have never shared your faith story with her so you are really not *doing* anything for God. If you really loved the Lord you would not even hesitate to share Him with her. If you *really* cared at all about your aunt you would have shared with her years ago. You are such a loser. I doubt if you are really a Christian at all!" Before long you begin to buy the lies being spoken. Your discernment shot, you begin to feel depressed and full of despair.

At next week's demonic staffing the assigned culprit in your case has much to report to the superiors of hell. Without Divine intervention and knowledge of the promises of God you are spiraling downward, nearly out of control. You called off your luncheon and sulked in your bedroom for hours. But it did not have to be that way. You are a chosen vessel for God Almighty. The devil need not have this kind of access to your life. The demonic principle does not need to take root in you and it will not, provided you understand the powerful principle of God for your life!

Principle #2 - The call of God is greater than the fall of man!

Because the devil is the chief liar and has lied from the beginning (see John 8:42-44), we need to see the pattern that started it all for humankind. The man, created in God's own image, in His likeness, male and female (See Genesis 1:27) they were made, falls prey to the temptation of the enemy. This temptation is made sweeter because of the liar's twisting of words. He poses a question, an accusation if you will. His statement, "God has not surely said..." begins to permeate the woman's mind. She thinks on these things for a moment or two (we are not sure how long, really) and then decides that something that looks good and smells good certainly cannot be all that bad. In reality the temptation was an implantation of the spirit of lust, a lust for what God alone possessed, the knowing of good and evil. Using the same argument that he tried before the throne, "For God knows that in the day that you eat from it your eyes will be opened and *you will be like God*, knowing good and evil" (Genesis 3:5), Satan wanted to be like God. He wished to be the object of worship and only the Lord was to be praised. After being cast from the presence of the Lord, the enemy has become bent on convincing people that they too can be gods. What an effective argument. There are complete groups of cults that believe that their destiny is to become gods! When woman ate of that tree mankind fell and experienced death. The devil had suggested, "You shall not surely die". What a liar!

Mankind fell, sinned against God and was found to be uncovered (naked) in the garden. But wait, it did not end there. God knew immediately what had happened. There was a large "thud" in Heaven and God came on the scene. As a matter of first priority God made a covering for the man and woman. Adam and Eve became the first recipients of divine grace. By the shedding of blood the Lord God made a covering from skin (Genesis 3:21) and the people were covered by the provision of the Lord. God's purposes will not be thwarted by the enemy's lies. His plan for mankind, for your life, will not be altered by the cunning craftiness of an angel gone bad. As much as the devil wants to think that he is some kind of superior being, the Lord has given us the ability to be overcomers in this life. God has effectively demonstrated time and time again that *the call is greater than the fall!* He has not forgotten a single promise that He has made to you. No matter how far removed from His purpose for your life you have removed yourself, God has made a way for your return and restoration.

Let us look at 2 Timothy 2:11-13 for a moment.

" It is a trustworthy statement: For if we died with Him, we will also live with Him; If we endure, we will also reign with Him; If we deny Him, He also will deny us; If we are faithless, He remains faithful, for He cannot deny Himself.

Dying can be healthy for us

When we come to Jesus Christ and confess our sin and then confess His provision for our lives personally something happens. There is a massive event in all of creation. God literally moves on our behalf. This change causes a major shift in our lives. We die, not a spiritual death, it is a death to the old nature that used to reign in us. We now live or rather Christ lives in us and we have the supernatural ability to overcome. We enter the "call" of God on our lives. We are destined to reign with Him!

Vessels of Wood or Honor?

When we were in our fallen nature we were like everything else that is dying. Wood is only good for a season. Earthen vessels will only last a certain amount of time. But we are called "vessels of honor"(see 2 Timothy 2:21). We have been set apart (sanctified) for a specific purpose. That purpose is to bring glory and honor to the Name of the Lord all of our days; when this life is over, we will bring honor to Him throughout all eternity.

Peter was a formidable figure among Jesus' followers. From

what we can gather the term "earthen vessel" likely applied to him quite well. A rough-hewn fisherman, quick with a temper and brave on the exterior while caving when it really counted, most of us can relate to this guy quite easily. Having denied the Lord Jesus, just as predicted, Peter finds himself face to face with His Lord in John 21:15-19. This discourse is amazing. Three times Jesus asks a specific question of the disciple, "Peter, do you love me?" Is it not interesting that there are three identical questions and three areas of "calling" that come following Peter's responses? Simon, son of Jonah had denied the Lord three times and the Lord issued a three-fold call to him. What a wonderful picture of restoration and redemption! Jesus declares to Peter that he is now "useful to the Master, prepared for every good work" (2 Timothy 2:21b).

Ask yourself this question, "Have I made room for all that the Lord would like to do in and through me?" Once we answer in the affirmative we will be on our way to becoming a vessel of honor unto the Lord. Do not allow your past failures, your past denials, your past sin, to disqualify you. The Lord has made a provision. He has chosen to cover you with His covering, by the blood of Jesus Christ, that you might honor Him all of your life. Once this begins to happen we become candidates for personal revival. We are on our way to becoming *radical vessels*. Get ready you are in for the ride of your life!

CHAPTER 6

Vessels of Revival

"The power is greater than the hour!"

For many years neither churches nor pastors would darken one another's doors to come together for anything more than a formal ministerial association meeting. The divisions were representative of doctrinal positions, styles of worship and the clerical clothing worn by pastors and priests. A religious hierarchy, although not formally established among the ministerial group, was very evident. The pastors of the larger mainstream denominational persuasion usually carried the most clout and held the executive positions in the club. Whenever anything of political and social importance was happening, the president or moderator of the group would appear publicly, get his picture on the society page of the paper with some government leader and would supposedly speak on the behest of the group as a whole.

The word "ecumenical" began to flow freely in the 1960's and there was a sudden urge to be seen as a part of one of these groups. There was immediately a great divide in a community. There were usually two very distinct and different associations. On one hand there was the more formal mainline denominational group, whose president was usually Presbyterian or Unitarian. In sharp contrast there was the "Evangelical" ministerium, with a Baptist or Free Methodist leader. It was very much an "us and them" thing. The definitions were quite clear. The mainstream group was *the* pastoral organization of the city, and the evangelicals were often thought of as the outside, radical, "fundy" faction. Pentecostals were nowhere to be found because their pastors were usually not educated in seminaries and their churches were small, insignificant and predominately poor congregations.

Crashing the party

As a young pastor in the late 1970's, I had been raised in a mainline denominational church. I was completely ignorant of the division that existed. So, shortly after being ordained in an independent charismatic church, I began to attend the pastors' Bible study at the large and prestigious Methodist church and paid my dues to become a member of the ministerial association. I never considered that my presence at those meetings was in the least controversial. I had graduated from a Bible college that had never been heard of, at that time had no seminary experience and had even been invited "out" of my former denomination by the assistant to the synod president, because I was a charismatic. I did not dress like a preacher, worked full-time in secular employment to support my family and basically did not fit the prim and proper concept of an uptown minister. Our meetings were generally boring. Our guest speakers at the monthly association meetings were usually not Christians but rather community and social service related guests who came to inform us about their agency and how we could refer our members for services. We had coffee and donuts, stood around talking about our churches and the attendance numbers. The meeting was called to order and the presiding minister would introduce our guest. After the meeting, each pastor went his own way and there was no relationship between us for the next month and all through the summer.

Now, do not get me wrong. There were good men and women involved in our group. There were even some friendships struck as a result on occasion. However, there was never any real impact on our city because we had met. Our members never did anything together, with the exception of a couple of small churches combining their summer Vacation Bible School programs. There seemed to be no real concern for souls and worship together was simply non-existent. I remember more than one "service of unity" in which there were more pastors present than congregants.

Let there be no divisions

Today across the land we are seeing pastors of all stripes, who love Jesus and His Word immensely, coming together to pray and seek God. There is an awakening for souls among the leaders of congregations, both small and large. However, in spite of these leaders coming together, even weekly, there remains a large chasm between Christians in general. There are still those who are totally committed to following after Pastor Peter, or Brother Apollos, or Rev. Paul. Even though the pastors themselves are committed to unity there is still not much vision for it in the pews. We still prefer our little prayer meetings and what *our church* is doing. We seem to remain convinced that for some reason the world will suddenly show up for our 10 a.m. service begging to become a part of what has been termed the most boring hour of the week! We are totally committed to the wrong things. Even in larger Full Gospel churches across the nation we see this "we have the corner market on all truth" syndrome, or what I prefer to call a "sindrome". Who on earth do we think we are? When did we become the owners of the house? Does not the Bible call us servants to the owner? What or who gave us the authority to promote this heresy? The more important question may be, "what are we doing about it?"

Backward is never forward

I believe that the primary problem is that we have gotten it all backwards. Someone, somewhere, came up with the idea that if we could just get pastors and church members to come together on occasion we could have revival in the land. But this concept does not appear in the scriptures. Additionally, it does not work! Mark these words carefully: *Unity does not bring revival...<u>revival brings</u>*

unity! I am so totally convinced that this is truth. Try as we may, putting a bunch of pears in with a basket of apples will not produce one kind or the other. We have lost sight of the tree from which we come! It is going to take some _radical vessels_ to get this thing straightened out. But even some radical (and biblical) movers and shakers will not get the right outcome if we are not filled with a power not of ourselves. I understand that the believers in Acts 2 assembled in unity <u>before</u> the outpouring of the Spirit. But I also understand that they had personal revival before they had unity. Jesus had spent time dealing with them individually, restoring their lives as it were before they could be unified in that upper room.

We have two specific examples of personal revival among the first disciples prior to the congregational unity of Acts 2:1. The first is Thomas, the doubter. Why did he question the validity of the resurrection? Was he a really bad guy and wayward follower? I think not. I believe that Thomas simply displayed his humanity and that humanity is shown to us for good cause. When we fall into seasons of doubt the Lord is faithful in spite of our unfaithfulness. He _is_ faith when we are faithless. Jesus restored Thomas in such a gentle and important way. He showed him the _reality_ of his scars and wounds. At the same time the Lord revealed His resurrection having the needy follower touch Him. O how we need to touch Jesus!

The next example is the most spoken of. He is Peter, the rock, the steady, brave, sword-wielding soldier of the cross, who caved like a sinkhole in a rainstorm when it really came down to it. Yet, on that early morning when the fisherman decided to do all that he knew to do…go fishing…Jesus came with His restorative power, revealed Himself to Peter and the others, and then gave Peter the charge to feed, care for and otherwise lead the sheep of His fold. Following this personal revival Peter and the others are found to be "in one accord, in one place" where the Holy Spirit is poured out upon them and the Church is birthed. Peter then preaches a message that leads about 3,000 men to Christ. Revival brings unity, which then returns the favor! This is a great concept, because it is a "God concept".

We are called to become vessels through which God can bring the spirit of revival. The hour that we live in demands that a people be raised up who will see that the Lord desires to pour out His Spirit upon all people (see Joel 2:28 NIV). Jesus has declared that the fields of this world are ready to be harvested and the need is for workers to harvest those fields. Many people simply do not believe that they can be accepted by the Lord or His Church. They have the impression that they must perform some special service or act to gain acceptance. They are convinced by what they see and hear that there is really no room for them. They are ready to be harvested, but there are not many who are willing to invite them to the table.

For many years Christians have mistakenly thought that inviting people to attend church was the answer. After all, they presumed, it is the preacher's job to win the lost, not ours. All we need to do is get them to the gathering and they will get the message. While to some degree this may work, it is hardly the intent of our Savior that His body would be so sublime and bland about going after the harvest. The great commission involves every believer! The call to be "preachers" of the Word belongs to all who have come to the saving knowledge of Christ. The Holy Spirit will equip each one who asks to be used of God to promote the Kingdom. We must get this straight: pastors and church leaders are not the only ones with a call! The anointing of God to take the gospel to every creature belongs to the whole body and everyone has an important assignment right in front of them. Someone made some "rules" about proper church etiquette and forgot to ask the Lord about it!

A *radical vessel* is one who knows that the power of God is greater than the hour in which we live. In spite of all of this unbiblical religion there is still truth. The Word of God gives us this truth. Today the Body is fragmented, each going his or her own way and there is not much real direction being given. When was the last time you heard a sermon about the call on every believer and then had the pastor teach and release everyone to his or her calling? I have been quite tempted lately to have a "mass ordination service." I am sure that this would raise a few eyebrows and maybe even get some press attention. I was thinking that I would stand in front of the congregation and ask all of the believers in the house to stand. I would then raise my hands over them and declare them to be duly and properly ordained to the ministry! After the great gasp clears the room and there are shouts of "heresy, heresy", I will explain that the Word of

God makes no provision for those occupying the offices of apostle, prophet, evangelist, pastor and teacher, to be the only "true" ministers of the good news. In fact, to the contrary, the Bible speaks of the priesthood of all believers, just as Martin Luther preached.

> *"But you are a chosen people, a <u>royal priesthood</u>, a holy nation, a people belonging to God, that you may declare the praises of him who called you out of darkness into his wonderful light."* (1 Peter 2:9 NIV)

Furthermore, the Word plainly tells us that "to each one is given a manifestation" of the Spirit (see 1 Corinthians 12:7). The Lord has decided that every born again believer in Christ is called to be a "preacher" of the Word of God. There are no exceptions to this truth. We may all *preach* in different ways, according the grace given us, but we must all preach! Unless and until the Body of Christ becomes awakened to this, embracing it and then being released into it, we will not be vessels of revival as we are intended to be. Leaders must stop hording the goods and claiming an ownership of that which belongs to the whole Church, and must begin to equip and release, which is the call upon the ministry leaders (see Ephesians 4:11-13).

We are in a vital hour. There is much evil working against the cause of Christ. But the power is greater than the hour. *Radical vessels* are being raised up in this last day. Are you one of them?

CHAPTER 7

Vessels of Purity

"The Blood is greater than the flood!"

I am sure that this chapter could really rock your boat if you let it. First, let me say that it is not my intent to bring something to you that would promote either of two extremes that have long existed in the Church. These teachings have elements of truth, but do not contain the totality of truth that sets the captives free…truly free.

Extreme proposition #1

This theory supposes that everything is really all right in the world and that there is no need to be concerned about holiness whatsoever. Jesus has paid the price. I cannot get holy enough for God. I will never cease from sinning. I am saved by grace through faith alone. So far, so good! Let us now take it to the "logical" place that it usually goes. Because I am saved by grace there is really no point in *trying* to live for God. I cannot do it anyway, so I will simply live my life, enjoy the fruits of my temporal labor, eat, drink and be merry, because when I die I am covered by a grace that supercedes my need to be right with God. Everyone is saved because a loving God would never send anyone to hell, right? I am not a bad person...I have never killed anyone....there are many paths to eternal life...Jesus is only one of those...I grew up in church...I went to Sunday School...I was baptized as an infant...I really do not *need* to do anything!

Extreme proposition #2

I know that Jesus died for me. His blood has covered my sin. I am a sinner and need His forgiveness and must ask for it in order to receive it. He is a holy God, Who requires holiness. I must be blameless in His sight. So far, so good! Now, let us go on to the place that many have taken it. My sin has separated me from God and the Lord requires that I do some things in order to get that which He offers. I must leave my old life behind and do my very best to come to Christ. If He will have me I will be saved. Once I am born again I will need to strive toward the perfection that will cause my sanctification. After I have achieved this holiness, I will no longer sin. I will be totally righteous and not have the current struggle that I have. In order to get to this point of righteousness, I will need to clean up my life. It will be a struggle, but I think I can, I think I can, I think I can!

These two extremes have long created an unbiblical myth about the Lord. In the first case we fall into the worldly religion of universalism or the idea that all will be saved in that day, if there is a day, and that God has simply redeemed everything by His love. There is just enough truth mingled with this position to make it very attractive. It presupposes that God would never subject any of His creation to judgment. Equally this position makes a claim that if I simply live a nice clean life God will have to recognize that I am basically good and deserve to be in Heaven when I die. After all, anything else would simply be unfair.

In the second theology we create an equally mythical God who responds to our good works as though they somehow qualify us for Heaven. If we clean up good enough to come to the Lord so that we will be acceptable to Him, He will respond with His favor and give us a place in His presence...at least until we screw up again...then

He will condemn us and send us packing.

The problem with the first example is that there is nothing required on our part whatsoever. This simply does not fly in the face of the scriptures. Coming to the Lord is a basic requirement of the Word of God. Jesus did not say that whether we came personally to Him or not He would save us. He did say, *"Come unto me..."*

Perhaps our primary problem is our definition of faith. Instead of choosing a path of understanding faith we have simply defined it as belief. The problem with this view is that it does not consider the activity that faith involves.

Hebrews 11:1 states that, "...faith is the substance of things hoped for and the evidence of things not yet seen." Substance and evidence are important words and by implication are more active than simply believing. The Bible tells us that even the demons *believe* (see James 2:19). No, faith has more elements than simple belief.

Repentance. One implication in *faith* in Christ is that we are required to turn from something toward something. This is called repentance. John's message was repent for the kingdom is at hand (Matthew 3:2). Jesus then followed with the word "repent" (Matthew 4:17). Then the Church is birthed and one of the first words uttered by Pastor Peter was "repent" (Acts 2:38).

Trust. Faith involves no longer trusting our ways and means and giving ourselves confidently to reliance upon the Lord. Psalm 20:7 puts it this way: "Some *trust* in chariots, and some in horses: but we will remember the name of the LORD our God." (KJV)

Confidence. If we attempt to add anything to what the Blood of Christ has provided we fail to place our whole life into His hands. Our confidence will not be in Him but in ourselves. Philippians 3:3 says, "for we are the *true* circumcision, who worship in the Spirit of God and glory in Christ Jesus and put no confidence in the flesh..."

Fruit. Faith produces results. Simply stated, if I am repentant, moving from an old life toward a new one, and am trusting in the Lord confidently there will be a result. We have been created in

Christ to bear fruit. Jesus prayed that we would bear fruit. Hebrews 11 shows us the fruitful lives of those who placed their hearts in the hands of the Lord.

Faith *is* believing, but it is more than simply believing.

This is why it is so powerful. It is why faith can move interminable mountains. It is why it overcomes the worst of the worst: sin. When our faith connects with God's mercy and grace that which is produced is nothing less than purity.

We are called to be vessels of purity. However, we cannot and will not realize this purity in our own strength. It is clearly and only by the Blood of Jesus Christ shed on the cross for us that produces any holiness that will be able to stand in the presence of the Lord.

Many lives have been inundated or flooded with sin and perplexity. Bad decisions abound. Leaning on what we understand to be true rather than what is really true always produces a flood of frustration. In his dissertation on the "State of the Godless" Job tell us in chapter 27:20, "Terrors overtake him like a flood; a tempest steals him away in the night." Faithlessness produces fear and it comes in like a flood to those who only trust in themselves or in other humans or institutions. If we are to be *radical vessels* we must come to rest in the provision of the Lord for our purity. He is the One who makes us holy. His Blood covers the many sins that have prevented us in the past but provide for us when we enact our faith in Him. The process that brings us to this attitude of faith is called *preparation*. How prepared are we?

CHAPTER 8

Vessels of Preparation

"More oil, less toil!"

The age-old pledge of the Boy Scouts says, "Be Prepared". Yet most believers in Christ have little, if any, concept of what it means to be "instant in season and out of season". For many years now we have heard sermon after sermon on the merits of getting ready for something...but what? What are we preparing for? Usually the message deals with being ready for the return of Christ. I have met many Christians who toil greatly over whether or not they will be in good enough favor with God to actually make the rapture! I have even heard some say that if you do not believe in the rapture you will be left behind! How absurd, especially when one considers that this particular end time teaching is a very recent addition to the theological bookshelves.

  Please do not misunderstand, I am not advocating for any specific eschatology. On a personal note I do not spend much time on "last days" issues, because they are very much a mystery that I have not been led to teach much about. I do believe in the personal return of Jesus Christ, and that it is near. St. Paul also believed this, as did the other members of First Church. No, what I am teaching about in the area of "preparation" is a readiness in Christ today. Are we in a place of being able to respond for the Kingdom regardless of what comes? This is so vital a message today. We are called to be "shod with the *preparation* of the good news concerning peace" (see Ephesians 6:15). While this is not a book about the controversies of pre, mid, post or no tribulation positions, it is about getting ready for something. We are called out from something toward something...and I think that *something* is really big! God is looking to change us and to get us ready for a divine appointment in this earth. He is seeking vessels willing to be used by Him to reach the lost with the gospel. While we await whatever is next in the "God calendar" we must be working while it is yet day (see John 9:4). The real question is, "Will the Son of man find faith in the earth when He returns?" (Luke 18:8 paraphrase). I interpret this passage to mean that when Jesus comes, anytime Jesus comes, He is looking for us to be *about* something that He has ordained for us to do.

And yet so many attempt to do the works of the Father by their own abilities and might. The temptation to do mighty exploits from this human strength is so embedded in the lives of people, all of us! As the plans were being drafted to resurrect the city of God following seventy years of captivity, there appears to have been an attempt to engage in the work without the direct supernatural involvement of God. At the very least the Lord prophetically warns those builders to not attempt such a disgraceful act when through Zechariah's prophecy He says, "Not by might, nor by power, but by my Spirit, says the Lord of hosts" (Zechariah 4:6).

How do we cease from the frivolity of our attempts to "do more" "be more", and "get more done" in our own vitality? I submit to you that the Lord has given us the full answer. He has imparted something to true believers in Christ that no man can take away. He has offered an ability that is far beyond our own fragile frames.

For far too long much of the Church has rejected the oil of God's Holy Spirit, largely due to fear or misunderstanding or even the errors of those who have claimed to have had "it". Because some have attempted to use the things of the Spirit for their own personal agendas some believers have done everything except stand on their heads and spit nickels to keep Christians from walking in the fullness of the Holy Spirit, Who is God Himself. With theological elasticity these fearful teachers have stretched the tried and true interpretive methods of old to keep their people from experiencing a freedom and power that the leaders might find *hard to manage*. "Management" may very well be the problem!

    I have made the following observation many times. It is not intended to be of a critical spirit in the least, but a simple observation over twenty-five years of ministry: church leaders are some of the most insecure people on earth! Why? I am sure that there are many possibilities, perhaps as many as there are leaders. This insecurity, whatever its root, bears some striking fruit. It usually appears in the form of "control". Insecure leaders are control freaks! This presents a clear and present danger regarding encouraging Christians to go after the oil of the Spirit.

    Many believers who have claimed to be "baptized in the Holy Spirit" have turned into rebels rather than revolutionaries. The rebellious spirit is not of God. Another common attitude that Spirit-filled believers seem to appropriate is what I call the "corner market syndrome". It is the perspective that says, "I've got something you don't have" and you can almost hear the juvenile tune that accompanies the lyrics! While the Charismatic movement of the 1960's up to the present time has brought some much needed truth to the Church, it has also been the seedbed of some quite serious striving and out and out divisiveness. So, the tendency of insecure pastors, who have a control problem, is to "throw the baby out with the bathwater". Interesting phrase, is it not? It comes from a time when bathing was a privilege only experienced occasionally, perhaps even annually! The first to bathe was the head of the house, the father. Then the mother would have her turn, and subsequently the remainder of the family until finally (in the original water – ugh!) the baby of the family was bathed and the nearly blackened water discarded. The warning was intended to save the baby's life by not discarding the tot with the murky mud of the annual baptism. Unfortunately, many pastors and church leaders decided that this was not a problem. They simply chose to either ignore the Third Person of the Trinity or relegate Him to the status of an "it" and stretch the Biblical text as far as possible in order to avoid the possibility of having to deal with the occasional spills in aisle 12!

The other problem came when pastor/teachers became fearful of confrontation. So rather than deal with the false prophet or wolf in the midst (ignoring the command of the Word to guard the flock – See Acts 20:29-31), leaders become "chickens" and now we have intimidated, control freaks, who bend the Word to fit their purposes, and fail in one of the most warned of instructions in the Bible to "not quench the Spirit" (1 Thessalonians 5:19).

We need the power and provision of the Holy Spirit today more than ever before. We also need more teaching on the truths of God's Word regarding the Spirit. We must somehow recover that which the enemy has stolen from the Church concerning this matter. Just because some denominations have placed an improper emphasis on a particular gift or usage does not mean that the whole thing should be dismissed. God has given His Spirit for many reasons. Jesus baptizes in the Holy Spirit for good cause…without this outpouring we will soon be operating in our own strength and effort. We will forget that this Christianity stuff is supernatural stuff. It will quickly become about us rather than about Him! We <u>must not let that happen any longer!</u>

I have a call to issue forth to all who have been filled with the Holy Spirit and proclaim the Baptism in the Spirit to others…get it right! Preach the power of God for living and for taking the gospel to the world. Stop majoring on the minors and get with the biblical program. Go back to the Word of God and get a fresh thing happening in your life. To whom much is given much is required!

I also have a strong word for those who have rejected Him. Repent! You are quenching the Holy Spirit. He is God and He will not tolerate your bad theology long. Stop being fearful and controlling. Your ministry is not your own…it belongs to the One Who called you! You, too, must go back and study the Word in a fresh way and open yourself and your congregation to what the Lord is doing in this hour.

Ten Virgins – five quarts short!

You may not agree with my interpretation of Matthew chapter 25…but this is my book so I am going to give you my view on it anyway! It is really quite simple. First, let me tell you that I am not taking an eschatological view of this chapter...you are free to if you must...but for this lesson I am not.

Here is the equation: ten virgins – ten vessels of lamp oil - five wise or prudent - five foolish. What made the first five prudent? They *took oil with them*. What made the other five foolish? (Get ready this is really, really profound!) *They did not!* Read it carefully...do not get too hung up about the return of the bridegroom in this parable...just let it sink in. Half of them (all of them young women, as the Greek calls them. Not a single one of them turned into an ape or a man, they remained women, all ten of them!) had oil with them, and half of them did not. The latter half went to light up and could not, so in their own strength they came to the sisters of prudence (who were lit up at the time, shining brightly). Unfortunately, time had run out and they missed the opportunity, as it were.

Now be really careful here. The issue is in whose strength do you choose to walk? Do you choose to make it with your own wisdom, power and excellence, or do you *choose* to function in the power of His might (see Romans 15:19)? To be a *radical vessel* you will need to take the risk of "losing control". But if you are willing to release full control to the Lord of Hosts you will no longer be operating from your own strength base. You will know what you have longed to know. Fear will no longer consume you, for you will only know the fear of the Lord, where wisdom begins (Proverbs 1:7). Your own head knowledge will simply not do any longer. To be a *radical vessel* you will need to cease the striving (toil) and obtain more of the Spirit of God for your life (oil). Less toil, more oil. You are now becoming a "Vessel of Preparation". God will use you to bring His message of restoration to a generation that will soon find a hunger to be restored!

CHAPTER 9

Vessels of Restoration

"What goes up – comes down!"

The ministry of reconciliation and restoration has long been a passion of mine. In 1989 my wife and I began Restored Ministries as a teaching arm of our work, focused on the reclamation of people for the Kingdom. We had discovered that many people, for one reason or another, had become discouraged, disenfranchised and disconnected from the Body of Christ altogether. The more we took the message of restoration to various churches the more we discovered a deep seeded problem. People did not understand the great price that has been paid for their very lives, and furthermore did not grasp the view that God had toward them. Pastors and leaders were no longer in ministry, some due to personal failures, others because they had become frustrated by the seeming pettiness of the politics of church life. Having gone through some pretty serious problems myself in this regard, I felt a particular need to find the truth of the Word of God concerning restoration.

Certainly it could not be that the very God who imparted gifts and callings into the lives of men and women would simply discard these same people because they had displayed their clay nature and been sidelined for a season. Surely there had to be a better answer than suggesting that one who had failed, sinned or fled should give up altogether and never, ever, serve the Lord or His people again. The more I studied the Bible the more I noted that many, if not most, of those who God had used in major ways had themselves been given to serious error or frustration or even worse in their lives. But I noticed that nearly to a man (or woman) God had a plan that would bring them back and subsequently restore them to a fully functional and, might I add, successful place in His Kingdom.

In making the above statements I must clarify some things. In virtually all cases of biblical restoration there was 1) repentance on the part of the fallen one; 2) a period of "shelf time" that was usually in a wilderness of sorts; and 3) a restored ministry that was richer and fuller than had ever been known before. The other most notable thing that I discovered was that those who had come through the wilderness season, whether they were there due to their own problems or those put upon them by others or even by God Himself, permanently had a heart to restore others who were being inflicted in the same ways. I am reminded of the scripture found in Luke 12:48 (my paraphrase), "Whomever is granted much shall be required to grant that much more". I know that I am lifting the text from its proper context, but just consider the reality of this truth. God has a serious expectation of those that have received much. We are required to give away that which we have received!

I wonder if Peter would have been so open to the ministry to the oppressed and abused if he had not denied Jesus thrice? I have some doubts if Paul's attitude toward his enemies would have been redemptive, as it often was, had he not been a persecutor before being persecuted. I have met many pastors who have experienced personal failure (not particularly what you are thinking, either) and following their wilderness experience become more tender, merciful and graceful toward others. I know that this is my experience. My tolerance toward those who are in need of restoration is much higher and broader today than it was, say 20 years ago, when I "had it all together and knew everything"! Having been broken, disappointed, hurt and even cast aside, and subsequently restored to a ministry greater than any I could have imagined, I have a burning passion to see people come through their bad times into the best times.

If the earthly ministry of Jesus Christ was not actually focused on the wayward people in need of forgiveness and reconciliation, than what was it principled upon? It does not take a PhD in Middle Eastern cultures and religion to plainly see that Jesus spent a lot of time with the "sinners" of His time. If you wanted to locate the Son of God on any given day, just look for where the thieves (tax collectors), prostitutes and throwaways were. Most of the time He was with them. Interestingly, Jesus was not summoned to come to the scene of the woman caught in the act of adultery. He was apparently close by! If you listen carefully as you read the gospels you will hear Jesus speaking rather harsh words to the crowd at times. But those words were not at the "sinners" of the time. Rather, these words of conviction were leveled at the religious leaders, the pastors and bishops, of the day. He told sinners that they needed to cast their cares upon Him. He called the leaders hypocrites and whitewashed tombs!

> *"Woe to you, scribes and Pharisees, hypocrites! For you are like whitewashed tombs, which on the outside appear beautiful, but inside they are full of dead men's bones and all uncleanness. "So you, too, outwardly appear righteous to men, but inwardly you are full of hypocrisy and lawlessness."* Matthew 23:27,28

So what is restorative ministry about? What does it mean to be restored? How do we become vessels of restoration in a time where there is so much lawlessness and sin? How do we conduct ministry that leads people to finding their true worth in Christ?

Is the Church ready to be restored?

Much of the Church may not even recognize the need to be restored. After all, we are functioning quite fine doing it our way. We have established hierarchy that does not even come close to the New Testament pattern for the Church. There are many people within the Church that seem to have no role whatsoever. Many are in a "Corinthian" state in this hour. They are followers of men's ministries. They are competitive with one another in a very worldly way. There seems to be no room for correction and discipline. The gifts of the Holy Spirit have been ignored, preached against, or abused for selfish reasons. There are many false prophets in the land, who are not submitted to godly authority and a sense of superiority has again entered the Church's leadership. We desperately need restoration and do not even know it! You cannot get more lost in direction than this. The word "servant" is tossed around as though it is really happening, when in many cases it is not. Whether or not the Body of Christ is ready for restoration, it is in need of it. Once we embrace true restorative ministry we will be ready to impart it to virtually every part or member of the Body.

A simple look at the Book of Acts will give us a working model for the Church. It is this aim that I believe we must take. While making some cultural adaptations we must have the "spirit" of the Church in Acts. What are the characteristics of the New Testament Church?

While there was a strong authority, it was true authority.

The leaders of the fellowship of believers spoke with authority and functioned in the same power as Jesus had. It was a "servant authority" because these pastors and leaders knew that the Church belonged to the Lord and not them. When there were signs and wonders following the word preached, it was of compassion and not show. The only indication of elevating leaders to an improper place was from the people, according to what the Bible teaches us. You do not find letters addressed to pastors and bishops dealing with putting themselves on pedestals. You *do* see Paul redressing the issue of elevating the view of leaders among the Christians at Corinth. This is because, from what we know, the leaders were committed to serving people, loving Jesus and preaching the Word of Life. The authority of these leaders was true authority because the same thing that motivated the Lord Jesus, a serious compassion for the people, the lost and the saved, motivated it.

The early Church and its leaders were committed to seeing the Church grow through evangelism.

It becomes apparent from the birthday of the Church that there always remained one important mission and that mission captivated every fiber of the believers' lives. They were totally sold out to the Great Commission of Christ – to seek and save that which was lost. Unless and until the Spirit-filled Body of Christ is restored in this area numeric growth will always be hollow. While it is true that many Christians have been led to leave dead formalism to come into the life that is found in a vibrant church, it is vital that the Church become soul winning again.

The early Church and its leaders were committed to restoring broken lives.

Poverty, rejection, persecution and sin abounded in those days *and* in our times too. There is such a need to reach people with the good news that Jesus will not discard those who call upon Him. He will not forsake those who cry out to Him and He will always provide His manifest presence to those who seek His face. We must become vessels of restoration.

So, where do we begin? It all starts with *reality*. In John 4 Jesus speaks to a Samaritan woman who was living in sin. The Lord chooses this moment in time and this particular sinner to reveal a most important truth. God is seeking worshippers. Not only that, but God is seeking those who will worship Him in spirit and truth. Another way of putting it is that God will respond to and chase after those who are being real in their approach to Him. This reality will bring us to our faces before Him. We will become humble in His presence and then the restorative processes will begin. Let us look at this powerful truth from the first letter written by Peter, the one who knew personal restoration in a powerful way:

> *"Humble yourselves, therefore, under God's mighty hand, that he may lift you up in due time."* 1 Peter 5:6 NIV

There is a call to humility. Under the watchful hand of the Lord, as we humble ourselves, God will "lift you up". Let us go on...

"And the God of all grace, who called you to his eternal glory in Christ, after you have suffered a little while, will himself restore you and make you strong, firm and steadfast." 1 Peter 5:10 NIV

The word translated "restore" in the NIV is translated "perfect" in other versions. The concept of being *perfected* is not one in which we somehow get so good that we can finally be established. No, we are perfected by grace through faith in the Lord Jesus and by humbly coming to Him. Although there may be hardships along the way God will *restore* and make you strong, firm and steadfast. The only requirement that is in our sphere of operation is that of becoming humble or real with God.

I submit to you that the Church is in need of restoration. The members of the Church are in need of restoration and the Church must begin moving in the ministry of reconciliation and restoration.

As our prayers and worship are birthed from humility, recognizing the greatness the power of the Lord, we will see His restoration and revival come down. It remains true that *what goes up comes down!*

CHAPTER 10

Vessels of Favor

"It's not what you know, it's Who knows you!"

"Remember me with favor, O my God." Nehemiah 13:31b NIV

Finding the favor of the Lord is a special thing. The problem comes when we begin seeking the favor rather than the "Favor Giver". But, still in all, favor is a really great thing. Whether it is favor from an employer as a result of hard work and effort, or from a family member recognizing the important contribution in relationship that has been made, finding favor is outstanding! Most people eventually learn, though, that you reap what you sow. When you sow favor toward others you will receive an abundance of it every time.

As Christians we are God's favorite. You see, the Lord does not have simply one favorite, but many. His house is filled with favorites. He loves all of His creation. "For God so loved the world that He gave…" His favor to us through Jesus Christ. Is it not really amazing how God loves us and has lavished upon us every good and perfect gift?

"In Him we have redemption through His blood, the forgiveness of our trespasses, according to the riches of His grace, which He lavished on us." Ephesians 1:7-8

We possess God's favor. He has decided to pour out such amazing goodness upon His children.

"Every good thing given and every perfect gift is from above, coming down from the Father of lights, with whom there is no variation or shifting shadow." James 1:17

But how did we come about deserving this favor? What made us so unique in the entire universe to be able to receive this abundant thing from God? The answer might surprise you. You might say, "Nothing! We are nothing and will always be nothing. This is totally a mystery." You would be both right and wrong at the same time.

First, it is true that we do not deserve anything from the Lord on the basis of what we have done. We are sinners, and if Christians, saved by grace through faith alone. However, God's view of us is very high. I know that many have heard that the Lord does not really see us as valuable, but that simply does not add up in light of the Word. God has spent the most valuable item that He possessed for us. He gave His one and only Son. Does this sound like someone who does not place a high value on humankind? In fact, God's primary interest is that the world would be saved through Jesus Christ (See John 3:17).

Take a look at Psalm 23, where the psalmist declares that God's goodness and mercy shall follow us all the days of our lives. This is God's favor. In Job 10:12 it says, "You have granted me life and favor and your care has preserved my spirit." Acts 2:46-47 says this:

"Day by day (the believers) continuing with one mind in the temple, and breaking bread from house to house, they were taking their meals together with gladness and sincerity of heart, praising God and <u>having favor</u> with all the people. And the Lord was adding to their number day by day those who were being saved."

It is clear from the Word that God's people are to be vessels of His favor and will know His favor and will impart His favor upon the earth. This will happen as we deliberately share His good news with all around us.

If we are to be *radical vessels* we will be recipients and imparters of God's wonderful favor.

Obtaining God's Favor

But how do we obtain this favor? I will list five ways to consider as a matter of lifestyle if we are to know the favor of God:

1. Humility – this word keeps coming up and for good reason. It is in the humble spirit that God will impart all of His goodness (see Micah 6:8).
2. Faithfulness – listening for God's voice and then responding to it. To know God's favor toward us we must make Him our favorite as well!
3. Endurance – run the race and do not give up until you have obtained the prize!
4. Pure motives – always check your reason for doing what you do. It our motives are not pure and glorifying to the Lord He has no avenue to work in and through us. We are simply in the way instead of being a party to His Way.
5. Servant posture – once we pick up the basin of water and wrap ourselves with the towel we are ready to "wash feet". Washing feet, so to speak, is the act of imparting the favor of God to others.

You may know a lot of things, but what you know is not nearly as important as Who knows you. It is important that we are known by the Lord and that He recognizes us as worshippers and vessels designed by and for Him. To be in the position to receive and subsequently impart His favor we must be in that place of relationship with the Lord God whereby He knows us, who we are and where we are. Once that fact is established He has promised to dwell in His house with His presence. If you are a Blood bought believer in Jesus Christ, you are that house!

CHAPTER 11

Vessels of the Presence

"With the story comes the glory"
"The manger is greater than the danger!"

Incarnation: in-kar-nā-shën \ noun 2. The union of divine and human natures in Jesus Christ (Merriam-Webster's).

> *"You will make known to me the path of life; In Your presence is fullness of joy; In Your right hand there are pleasures forever."* Psalm 16:11

> *"For You make him most blessed forever; You make him joyful with gladness in Your presence."* Psalm 21:6

> *"Surely the righteous will give thanks to Your name; The upright will dwell in Your presence."* Psalm 140:13

O how we love the presence of the Lord! The sweet, sweet presence of the Lord is so wonderful and we long to be in His presence. But we are called to a deeper truth. We are to be vehicles carrying the presence of the Lord. Jesus said that the Kingdom of God is with, or in or among men (mankind).

There has been considerable discussion concerning the issues of the presence and there are some really great definitions of the presence of the Lord that have been given by various authors and teachers recently. One of my personal favorites is that which distinguishes between the "omnipresence" of the Lord, His being everywhere all the time; and the "manifest" presence or the "glory" of the Lord. On one hand God, by His Spirit, is present everywhere and on the other He "shows up" at various times and seasons with a special demonstration of His power and might, perhaps in the form of signs, wonders and miracles. The Psalmist alludes to the first definition when he asks, "Where can I go that you are not there?"(See Psalm 139:7) A biblical example of the second understanding may be found in Ezra chapter one, where it says, "And the Lord stirred the spirit of Cyrus, king of Persia" (See Ezra 1:1). An even more demonstrative form of the "glory" of the Lord is found when the shepherds are visited by the angels or on the day of Pentecost, when the Holy Spirit is poured out on the Church.

In his book "Glory – when heaven invades earth" author Bob Sorge points out an interesting distinction between these two understandings of the presence of the Lord. In fact, Sorge gives four distinct usages of the word "Glory" in scripture as a noun, the fourth of which he describes as "The invasion of God's reality into the human sphere." It is this usage that I believe is what many if not most Christians who are in a serious relationship with Christ are looking for.

Notwithstanding the other applications, which are used more frequently in Scripture, this sense of the presence of the Lord invading our lives is intriguing and life giving for those who take worship seriously. It is this "presence" that once experienced becomes longed for. When we begin to know the Lord in this manifest way on a regular basis something begins to happen. For some it causes an unhealthy inward turn that if it continues will rob the believer of the great experience of "Vesselship". For most, however, the experience of Divine connection will cause us to become conduits of this precious presence of the Lord outwardly. For an example, I was greatly drawn to the deeper life in Christ by those who had experienced it. In a secular sense it is far easier to buy a car from someone who has driven the same make and model and has fallen in love with it than from someone who is just trying to get the car off the lot. The "sold out" salesperson is so turned on by his own experience that he cannot help but share the same with someone, anyone, and anywhere! When God's glory becomes reality to us we rarely want to hide that fullness. Instead we tell everyone around us about the wonderful expression of the Lord that we are experiencing, in the hope that they too will want to know the same kind of relationship with the Father.

But the glory of the Lord does not come to a person just because they want an experience. After all, this is the Lord of all Glory! To come to this place requires something of us. We are to seek Him if we are to find Him. Knowing someone who has received the benefits of the Glory of God and then attempt to obtain it by osmosis will not do. We must have a personal experience. In this life in Christ we are called to many personal encounters. Our hearts become full of the Lord as we seek Him (See Jeremiah 29:13-14). The requirement of every believer is to get so hungry for God that His Glory has to show up! It is in this pursuit of the Lord that we find His presence. It is in our passionate cry for more of the Lord that He meets us.

In the gospel of John chapter four the Lord says that the Father is seeking worshippers (See John 4:23b). Did you get that? God is *seeking* to join together with those who are *seeking* after Him! While He will not share His glory (credit, praise or honor) with anyone else (See Isaiah 42:8), He has created us to be a house filled with His glory (Isaiah 43:7). He desires to dwell in us and to reveal Himself to and through us.

Every situation that we face in this life is yet another opportunity for God to show up and reveal His Glory in us. We may be facing a very bad report or have just received some excruciatingly bad news...just another time for God to reveal His purposes and presence. He is building a life story within us and no matter how bad the story may sound to our ears, the Lord knows that if we will pursue Him passionately we will see His Glory in that pursuit. The Glory is greater than the story! The news may be bad but our God is great!

Jesus came as a baby in a manger. He could not have come otherwise. I have heard many preachers say that He could have come in any way that He chose to, but came as a baby. I do not think so! It was the Father's good pleasure to be incarnate in human flesh. It was His plan all along to come through a virgin girl and that He be born in a lowly place such as a barn and be raised in very "normal" surroundings. By being thusly born into this world the Son of God and Son of man demonstrated His humility and servant hood to all mankind. This low place that the Lord took was with a purpose. Ultimately the Lord would reveal His passion for the lost world that He entered by the cross. Furthermore the provision that was made in that barn that night would deliver all who call upon Him with a sincere heart. In this life we face many perils. Danger is all around those who trust in God. It has always been this way and will be until the return of Christ to reign. What we must remember, though, is that God has not forgotten us and has made the provision of His presence as it is needed. Remember: *The manger is greater than the danger!* The Lord's provision and promise is ours in Christ. He has called us to be *Vessels of His Presence* and thereby know His Glory in our lives. He then takes the willing vessel and uses it to reveal His love to the world. "We are His workmanship, created in Christ Jesus for good works." (Ephesians 2:10)

CHAPTER 12

Vessels of Purpose

"Different to make a difference!"

It does not take a rocket scientist to know that each and every person under heaven is totally and absolutely unique. Researchers and scientists alike have indicated that we possess different and specific DNA, fingerprints and other attributes that only belong to us. Still much of the church does not recognize these differences in human beings as being as valuable as does God. The Lord created us with different personalities, callings and gifts, all designed and placed to bring about His purposes in the earth. These gifts and callings, as we will discover, are intended to prepare a bride for Jesus the Bridegroom.

A Perplexing Problem

One of the most difficult problems that the church has faced in recent times is the desire of many to be seen as leaders and to hold and have positions of influence over others. There is an inherent problem in the human frame. Our nature is to be seen by others as important. Psychologists tell us that we need to have a sense of importance to be mentally healthy. Because of a "top heavy" structure in the modern day church we see many who have been catapulted to the "top" of the ecclesiastical structure and then have fallen a hard as they have advanced quickly. Ignoring a call to humility many have chosen a path that has led to their ultimate spiritual peril. Additionally, the church has been more than willing to place others on pedestals and lose site of the real purpose of ministry: to serve.

We *need* leaders. The Bible is very clear that God has given men in the form of government and leadership for the church to become all that it is intended to be. However, should the issue of leadership miss its primary purpose within the Body of Christ we are doomed to repeat again and again the mistakes of many before us. Ultimately we really *need* vessels in the church, radical vessels that will change nations with the message of the gospel of Christ. We need people who will come to the forefront and be functional regardless of what it may cost. The ministry is not about leaders, it is about every Christian finding his call, his purpose and then moving into that anointing even if it means losing everything that was once held dear.

The Ephesian Principle

Ephesians 4:11 marks a very important passage within the formation of the Church:

"And He gave some as apostles, and some as prophets, and some as evangelists, and some as pastors and teachers..."

Jesus Christ Himself gave these "offices" to the Church. Let us take a look at a plain understanding of what each of these did, based on their New Testament role, as we best understand it.

Apostle. The Greek word means simply, "One who is sent", but the actual function of this office is a whole other thing. The New Testament Apostle was one who established the Church. This was done, as we can see clearly in the lives of Peter, John and Paul, by preaching the Word, training and appointing others who would oversee the churches and by being led of the Holy Spirit in touching lives. Often we would see these apostolic leaders function in the miraculous and in healing ministry. Signs and wonders seemed to follow these men of God everywhere they went. Key words that could be used to describe "apostle" are: establish, oversee, train, demonstrate and lead.

Today the role of apostolic ministry has been viewed by many as the role of the missionary in establishing the Church in foreign lands. While this holds some truth it would be wrong to think that all missionaries do the work of an apostle. I submit to you that God is re-establishing the anointing of apostolic ministry in our time. It is being restored to the church with the same marks as that of the New Testament office. Those called to this ministry may or may not be in foreign lands. They are establishing, overseeing, training and leading by demonstration. In the eventual sense these leaders will function with signs and wonders following their work. These things will also follow those who are equipped by them for works of ministry.

Warning: The office of apostle is often abused and many have attributed to themselves the title without substance. Be aware that because we are in a title driven time in the Church many are enthralled with the concept of becoming an apostle. I think that they, as well as all of us, would do well to examine carefully the biblical admonitions of this call regarding humility, service and purpose.

Prophet. The prophetic ministry must reflect the "truly prophetic" and those who believe that they are called and given to the Church for the office must be willing to submit to the scrutiny of the Body in every way. In the 1980's and 90's we have seen a major push to accept this ministry as valid. This is a good and biblical thing. However, the abuses in this area have been devastating.

The office of the prophet is one that carries with it a real major responsibility to *truly* hear from the Lord and to impart that message, whether a declaration of present reality or a future revelation, to a church that is willing to judge the word and receive it if it is Godly, or reject it if it is not. Simply stated: prophets prophesy. They share the revelation of the Lord for the church. As with any office of ministry, if the people standing in that office forget that they are carrying a precious and awesome responsibility and thusly use the position to build "their ministry", they will become ineffective and even harmful to those around them. The prophetic anointing is a special place of standing and those therein must be faithfully committed to edify, exhort and comfort the Body of Christ.

Evangelist. We best understand this office by the life of the evangelist. Billy Graham comes to most everyone's mind. Others who are well known in this office are T.L. Osborn, Reinhard Bonnke, and similar figures. Those who define this role understand that theirs is the message of hope in Christ's provision for salvation. While all are called to evangelize there are those who stand in the office. Their passion is "souls" and they spend all of their waking moments carrying the "burden of the lost". One may say that this should be the burden of all Christians, and to an extent this is very true. However, the evangelist is also committed to equipping the Church to do the works of evangelism.

Pastor/Teacher. We think we know this office best and for obvious reasons.

The pastor has always been presumed to be the "authority" in the life of the local assembly. The pastor functions to shepherd or oversee the body to which he is assigned. In most cases it is understood that the pastor is the "full-time" employee of the church, therefore carrying the total ministry load of the fellowship. After all, that is why we pay him, right? The charismatic movement catapulted pastors into the limelight. Although there had always been the concept that the pastor was the leader (defining what a leader is will be very important to us as we study), the real understanding of pastoral ministry did not get much attention until this movement of the 1960's and '70's had come about. Unfortunately, the discipleship disaster came also. Pastors were thought of as nearly infallible and were placed in such high regard so as to rule over people in the church. There were people tithing directly to them, not making life decisions without their permission and even marrying only the person that the pastor determined to be the appropriate spouse! This type of demagoguery resulted in literal thousand of casualties. While there was much truth about issues of "spiritual authority" and "accountability" being taught, many of the "shepherds" forgot to read on about their real responsibilities to teach and release others into their destiny. They mistook the role of servant and turned it into a desire to be served.

One thing that did come from the renewal was the emphasis that pastors are also to be teachers. The Ephesian passage seems to indicate in its original language that the office is actually that of "pastor-teacher" and not two distinct offices of eldership ministry. Be that what it may, today we better understand that the pastor is simply one of at least four offices of eldership that carry a specific responsibility and concern.

The Rest of the "Ephesian Principle"

Ephesians 4:12-16

> *"...For the equipping of the saints for the work of service, to the building up of the body of Christ; until we all attain to the unity of the faith, and of the knowledge of the Son of God, to a mature man, to the measure of the stature which belongs to the fullness of Christ. As a result, we are no longer to be children, tossed here and there by waves, and carried about by every wind of doctrine, by the trickery of men, by craftiness in deceitful scheming; but speaking the truth in love, we are to grow up in all aspects into Him, who is the head, even Christ, from whom the whole body, being fitted and held together by that which every joint supplies, according to the proper working of each individual part, causes the growth of the body for the building up of itself in love."*

The calling is specific. All of the eldership gifts have one thing in common, they are given to the church to fulfill a mission: to bring the church into unity, maturity and ministry. This is even more important: the Church belongs to Christ. He is its head. We, leaders included, are a part of the Body, no more and no less. Unless and until leaders understand that to lead is to serve and to equip is to release, the Church will remain stagnant, compromised and woefully inadequate to carry out the mission assigned by Christ to her.

The *Real* Issue for Radical Vessels

We must understand that the Church is God's vehicle to saving the world, so to speak. Anytime that the Church has become focused on itself rather than the world around it, there has been birthed within it a myopic vision that has resulted in casualties. Unless each and every part of the Body is functional we cannot and will not be the full expression of the Lord God in the earth. Our message will become self-serving and the true vision of the Lord will be lost. God is calling for more than just ministry gifts to come forth in this hour. Radical vessels encompass all who deliberately run to God.

Other Vessels of Purpose

If the Ephesian gift of eldership are not augmented and supported by specific focus gifts they will soon become dry and unfruitful. Each one, whether it is the apostle, prophet, evangelist or pastor/teacher, must seek God to know their underlying appointment. Romans 12 speaks of these support ministries of purpose. They are found in verses 6 through 8 and include prophesying, serving, teaching, encouraging (or exhorting), contributing to the needs of others, government and mercy. These seven things are represented in each Christian's life call, whether in eldership ministry or not. But if one is in eldership one of these gifts will become evident. Additionally, each member of the Church has within himself the potential for ministry that is supported by one of these gifts.

A friend recently showed me this connection. Some pastors, for example, get focused on governing when their true gifting is in teaching or prophesying. While this does not preclude the biblical requirement of the overseer to oversee it may lessen the abilities that God has placed in the fellowship for government. As a result there is no room for the others that God has placed within that particular body to be functional. While there may be many in the midst that are gifted to lead in particular areas they are suppressed from doing so because the pastor is doing it all! In other words, the pastor may not be leading, but directing. For another example, there are exhorters within the church fellowship, but the only one who encourages anyone is the pastor. This ought not to be. The key is finding your underlying, or motivational gift and tuning in, thereby permitting others to take their assigned place within the fellowship. This provides the much needed balance that God has ordained for the Body of Christ.

"Are all apostles? Are all prophets? Are all teachers? Do all work miracles? Do all have gifts of healing? Do all speak in tongues? Do all interpret? But eagerly desire the greater gifts" 1 Corinthians 12:29-31 NIV.

The Church consists of *radical vessels* on assignment. If leaders wants to have the fullness of the move of the Lord in the midst of the assembly they will need to be ready to equip every part for their role.

Many people leave their particular fellowship because they don not feel "needed". Some of this is simply selfish ambition among the immature. However, some of it is because they are not being equipped to fulfill their destiny within that body. Pastors would do well to shepherd people into their callings and then make room for their gift to strengthen the church. Insecurity often prevents this, but it should not be so. I want to encourage every pastor and leader: be diligent to build the Kingdom rather than prevent it because you are afraid that someone will take over your turf! It is not your turf to begin with. It belongs to the One Who paid for it with His blood.

I also wish to encourage the church member: you are important and it is vital that you find your place and prepare your heart to be all that God has designed you for in the context of the church fellowship. Be careful…you must remain submitted to God's structure of things. But also be aware that God has a reason for having called you into His grace. He wants you to be a *radical vessel* for His purposes and not your own!

CHAPTER 13

Vessels of Completion

"The race isn't over until you hit the finish line!"

In the introduction to this book I spoke of the concept of seasons. I feel the reality of this issue all the time. As a pastor I have found myself trying to keep something going that seems to be losing its momentum. Not long ago, after our fellowship experienced several years of unabashed renewal and growth, there was a sense that we had cooled down a bit (actually more than a bit, but its hard to say that!). What my flesh began to do was nearly catastrophic. I thought, "My goodness...what do *we* need to do to get back what we once had?" For several days I moaned before the Lord, crying out for a methodical answer to what I perceived as a major dilemma. "God", I would say, "why are we so 'flat' in our affect right now? What do we need to do, what do we need to implement to get this thing back to where we were when renewal was all around and revival seemed imminent?" I considered what national speakers I could bring back to our fellowship that would pump things up again. We had so many friends among the "elite" of the anointed. Most of these great men of God had been with us during our years of renewal. "If only brother so and so would come and provide the spark of revival once again, we could keep this thing going a bit farther." But how far was that? At what point did we all simply give up the ghost from sheer exhaustion? Then the Lord began to show me something about the way He concludes a matter. What He revealed to me may not set well with some, but when you think about it prayerfully and look at it historically there is great merit in my synopsis.

God created all things with seasons and created them in due season. Exodus 34:21 says, "Six days you shall labor, but on the seventh day you shall rest, even during the plowing *season* and harvest you must rest."

Leviticus 26:4 states, "I will send you rain in its *season*...". Psalm 1:3: "He is like a tree planted by streams of water, which yields its fruit in *season*." Ecclesiastes 3:1 states, "There is a time for everything and a season for every activity under heaven." Speaking of God Paul writes Titus in the first chapter, "...and at His appointed *season* He brought His Word to light...". Seasons are important to God and they need to become so to us.

God's seasons in nature

In nature God has demonstrated His theology of seasons. In the spring there is rain and planting takes place. In the summer there is sun and growing takes place. In the fall the plants begin to die and the harvest takes place. In the winter the ground rests and prepares for the next season of planting to resume in its proper time.

God's seasons in humanity

In humanity we see a similar picture. A baby is born and drinks its mother's milk. After a season of time more solid foods are introduced. Simultaneously the child begins to crawl, walk, talk and so forth. We would not hand the car keys to an infant and expect much. We would also not put the responsibility for a corporation on the shoulders of most teenagers either. But if the seasons of life are cultivated correctly the youth grows into a young adult and the duties increase and the person begins to find their "harvest season".

In spirituality God concerns Himself with seasons as well. A brand new covert to Christ is not ready for the weightier matters of the Kingdom. They are in need of milk first and then meat. They must learn at the "feet of the elders" and then, sooner or later, they will enter the season of fruitfulness and increase.

The issues of seasons are directly related to the "concept of completion". In each cycle of seasons there is a sense of completion. When the winter, or resting time, comes we are entering into the completion of the matter. That does not mean there is nothing beyond the completion! Spring is on the way and God will bring a fresh new "thing" as we are diligent to rest in Him when it is time to do so.

Just as we cannot rush the calendar seasons and get the desired results we must not attempt to do so spiritually, as individuals or the Church. We need to get concerned when we have no seasons of fruitful harvest, though, and must not get complacent whatsoever. At the same time let us be careful to not build a greenhouse to rush the processes of God. His timing is perfect and we must be willing to move in His time all the time.

A *vessel of completion* is a person "whose God is the Lord". This person is willing to seek the Lord in the times of dry wilderness, with constant re-evaluation, with a heart set toward God and an eye on the coming move of the Lord. If we plant too soon the crop will fail. If we delay the harvest it will go to seed and we will lose the crop that was intended. If we rest too long we will miss the opportunity that springtime brings. As *radical vessels* we must be ready to move, ready to wait, ready to receive and ready to rest. This will cause us to become vessels of completion.

Now, back to my story. After a long period of searching and seeking the face of the Lord, He pointed out several issues to me about what He wanted to bring in the life of our fellowship. It would require the implementing of surrender on the part of leaders and passion from all of us. What I had perceived as an "end" God determined to be a "pause". This brief season of reflection and contemplation resulted in a fresh move of God in our midst and brought us all to a new level in Christ. The intensity of the journey soon became the joy of the provision…in due season!

Waiting for the Seasons

There is a considerable period of time as we go through the seasons of our journey in Christ. We are never called to "do nothing", even in the winter. If all we do is sit back and wait for the snow to melt and the sun to shine we will not be prepared for springtime. In the summer we must refrain from trying to pluck the harvest. It is not ready yet! If we attempt to pick a vegetable before its time it will be useless. The same is true in spiritual matters. We must remain faithful in waiting. We must remain steadfast in the midst of the unfolding of the seasons. While we are waiting for the harvest we must continually insure that there is enough water provided to the "would-be" harvest. We need to pray down rain and sunshine; we must trust God in the midst of the unpredictability of the way the season may go. The Bible puts it this way:

> *"Let us not become weary in doing good, for in the proper time we will reap a harvest if we do not give up."* (Galatians 6:9 NIV)

There is no room for quitting in the midst of the waiting. We are aiming for completion and must keep our aim true.

Consistency is the Key

So what do we do while we are waiting? Again we look at the natural to find the spiritual application. You cannot water your garden once all summer and expect a fruitful harvest. You cannot plant beans this year and expect many to grow in next year's season. Occasionally a renegade tomato plant will crop up, this is totally grace! But the norm is that you will need to plant to get a harvest and if you do not, well, there simply will not be one. So while we enjoy the warmth of the wood stove in the winter we are ordering seeds for the spring planting. While we are basking in the sunshine of the summer we are planning our schedules around the coming harvest, so that we provide enough time to take the harvest and store it for the winter. I think that you get my drift, so to speak.

Radical Vessels

Laziness will not produce a thing. Slothfulness will result in a big fat zero! There is a biblical principle here. If a man does not work he does not eat, or in other words enjoy the harvest.

I am a bow hunter, an archer. I really enjoy shooting my compound bows. It is a great sport, whether one hunts or not. To prepare for the archery season a shooter will spend the summer at a range or in the back yard shooting again and again. From ten yards, fifteen yards and twenty-five yards, the archer perfects his skills to the point where he has a very small "grouping" of arrows on the target regardless of distance. Accuracy comes with consistency. You develop your specific style and find one that works and then you practice doing the same thing over and over and over again. The same is true for any sport or occupation.

Yet many Christians are inconsistent in their life in God. Only attending the gatherings occasionally and praying now and then, spending even less time in the Bible, they have a notion that God will somehow just supernaturally pour into them all that they need. They complain of spiritual disconnection with the church fellowship but make no investment of time or effort to get connected. Consistency does not exist. When this is the case the seasons go unnoticed and the dryness becomes dryer and the fruit that could have been simply withers away.

When an army goes to war it prepares for war. It trains and learns the enemy well and then is better prepared for the battle ahead. The soldier becomes proficient by doing the same thing over and over.

If musicians are to become skilled they must practice and practice until they are so tired of the song that they nearly lose their love for it. But they then bring it before the people and many are blessed, including the performers themselves, in the fruitfulness of their labor.

Come on vessels, you must aim for completion! You must hit the mark over and over. You must be willing to pay the price to get the product. You must get radical and passionate about this thing! Once we become radical, once we see the fruit, we will not often be tempted to simply quit again. We will not give up and God will come into us and fill us with His fruitfulness for His glory and honor!

CHAPTER 14

Vessels of Hunger

"Where's the beef?"

Proverbs 16:26 declares that, "A worker's appetite works for him, for his hunger urges him on." I believe that we are in a serious time of change in the Church. There is a marked hunger among many of our members today. They are not satisfied with the crumbs of religion, nor are they happy with leftovers. While they may be intrigued by the history of revival, it is only because they are passionate to see God's hand moving today. For those who have walked in this thing for a long season this can be rather frightening. For many years pastors from pulpits have warned us that we must not look back and use statements like, "We have always done it this way" or "We've never done it like this before." The time has now come, or is soon to be upon us, that we must make up our minds (I am speaking to those like me, who have been engaged in ministry for twenty years or more and have been involved with major moves of God) that God is again up to something and if we do not work with Him we will be left out of the picture altogether. Worse than this is the fact that many of us lead substantial congregations and if we do not move on they will not.

In the 1970's there was a popular commercial for a well-known hamburger chain that depicted an older woman and her friends standing at the counter ordering. When the senior citizen's meal arrived she looked in the bun and cried out that now infamous saying, "Where's the beef?" As we consider the cry of the heart of many Christians today the same question might be asked. We are wondering what has happened to the ministry of those who are called to bring us into the fresh things of God. They seem to have gone the way of the church past and have become glued to the former ways of doing things, ignoring the warning of the prophet to "forget the former thing" (Isaiah 43:18). We are not only urged but required to press into the new thing that God is doing and to do so every time!

I admit to some level of frustration in this. As a pastor I have worked with some degree of diligence to stay on top of things happening in the larger body of Christ. I have generally embraced most of the apparent new things going on and have rejected only a few, some even wrongly. But when some "younger" believers start the old "war song" of hunger that is not being met I get a bit defensive. I may comment that I have always tried to listen carefully to the Spirit and follow after what He is doing. However, as time marches on I too want the "beef". I am very interested in the full move of the Lord in this time. While I am totally unwilling to throw out the word of God, as some would have us do to embrace a feelings and emotion based move, I am simply not about to eliminate God's proven design for His Church as found in the Holy Book. His way remains the best way. But I am concerned that much of what we hang on to is simply based on our tradition, even in the Spirit-filled assembly. We have our "programs" and our "committees" that are hard at work. We embrace our "order" of things and do so with passion, much the same as the denominational folks before us. God does not particularly require that we throw out the baby with the bath either. He is looking for our hearts.

If God does not own my heart he does not have my worship! If my ideas and concepts, which may have been God birthed at one point, but have now become obsolete and stale, are not infused with the passion of God Himself, I am hanging on to "my" stuff rather than embracing His. Hunger cannot ever be satisfied with old bread or flat wine. When my hunger begins to stir a longing in my being I must look to the author of my faith and see what is going on. There are three passionate pleadings that I believe the Holy Spirit is making to the Church in this hour to prepare the bride for Jesus.

1. *Return to the word of God.* By this I am referring to the Bible. Spirit-filled Christians have often been accused by our evangelical counterpart as being a bit on the loose side with the Bible. I think that often we are guilty as charged. I do not mean to paint this with a broad brush, but let us face it, much of the present day "charismatic" thing has been found to be in error. We have so called prophetic people out there who are not submitted to God's order or to any accountability at all. They continually make statements that prove to be wrong and are not called to give an explanation. They are rarely brought under biblical discipline, primarily because they are not a part of a local assembly, have no spiritual father and if they are confronted they often leave where they are shaking the dust from their sandals and scribing "Ichabod" over the door of the local church that has *rejected* them. They are often a sorry lot, always walking in a spirit of rejection and judgment. [It is good to note here that there are also many right-on prophets in our time, who are in submission to authority and are in solid accountability relationships. I call on them to spread the word among the others that this is both biblical and accurate. While these "big name" prophetic leaders may not realize it, there are multitudes of local churches and pastors who have been detrimental affected by wayward "prophets" who have rejected the scriptural model and brought much harm.] <u>We must get back to the very word of God</u> if we are to know truth. And we must know the God designed order for the Church and then operate in it.

2. *Pastors and other leaders must prepare for a change.* Change is coming. It must in order that we may conform to the heart of the Father concerning His Church. We must ask

ourselves what made the church in the book of Acts function so well and have such a powerful presence of the Lord that people were saved, healed, delivered and changed forever. What made these people willing to give up everything they had worked a lifetime for so that the poor among them could be blessed? I believe that the body of Christ is in for a major change in the very near future. We must begin now to change our thinking so that God can have His way in this closing hour of history.

3. *The Fruit of the Spirit will again become the fruit of the Church.* Those who are growing impatient with their churches or their leaders must become focused on their own attitudes. They must learn how to wait on God and have confidence in His provision *if they are walking with leaders who articulate a desire to move on with God.* God is way more patient that are we! He knows that He is working with human vessels. At the same time, *the Holy One of Israel will no longer tolerate compromise!* God is not going to stand back and permit His appointed leaders to lead people down the path of unrighteousness. He is not going to allow the false message of tolerance to be present in what is called His Church much longer. While true believers will begin to manifest love, joy, peace, patience, kindness, goodness, faithfulness, gentleness, and self-control (Galatians 5:22-23), He is calling His people to *return to their first love, resist the teachings of the Nicolaitans, no longer tolerate Jezebel, the spirit of death and dead religion, and make up their minds to no longer be lukewarm* (Revelation 2-3). That the Church is called to bear much fruit is a foregone conclusion (John 15:1-11.

We still have yet to address the issues of spiritual hunger in this hour. At the same time I feel the need to address some of the ongoing problems that the traditions of man have produced. I will focus on the latter first.

When I was first called of the Lord to the ministry I was a Lutheran. I have a deep appreciation for my roots in the local church in which I was raised. Although we did not hear much about Jesus from the pulpit, we did have godly Sunday School teachers that brought us the Bible. I was blessed to have a born again, Spirit-filled pastor when I was born again. Although I had never paid attention to the term "born again" and to my recollection do not recall ever being invited to a personal relationship with Christ in my home church, God interrupted my life at age twenty-one and I was radically saved.

My pastor then led me to the fullness of the Holy Spirit. He had recently become baptized in the Spirit and was a part of the charismatic renewal in our synod. Shortly after my conversion I felt a desperate drawing to serve the Lord and my pastor explained that this was a call to the full-time ministry. The requirement? I was called upon to get a four-year college degree and then enroll at an acceptable seminary of the denomination. After I had received my MDiv degree I could become a candidate for a pastorate. Once "called" by a church to be its pastor I would be ordained to the ministry. However, something just did not seem right about all of that for me. By this time I became "hungry" for God's word. I also latched hold of my "Lutheran roots" and took seriously the priority of the Bible that was decried by Luther himself. Unfortunately, my leaders in the denomination of which I was a part did not share this same passion. I recall one meeting that concluded my participation in active Lutheranism. This meeting was to pre-enroll at Gettysburg Theological Seminary. The man I met with began asking me about my "charismatic tendencies". I could not, nor would not deny what the Lord had done in my life. The result was that I was invited "out" of the church. I have no regrets over this, as the Lord has given me great grace since and I have looked back on the incident as a God thing in my life. Why this story? Because much of the church has failed to realize that it is vital to follow God's direction regarding the training of leaders.

The Spirit-filled circles, in many cases, have come to believe that all we need is "anointing" and that that better leaders are ones not formally trained. This is just plain wrong in light of the word of

God. At the same time there are those who are looking for titles that come with education and degrees. This is equally false. I agree with a statement once made by Rick Joyner. He stated that some are called to gain more training because the Lord would use them in the training of others; while others would only be required to receive certain training pertinent to their particular call. I am one of those who has been called to train others, so more training has been required for me. I do not wear that as a badge of honor, but a prerequisite for the job, so to speak. All are called to study (2 Timothy 2:15) and become proficient in the word of God regardless of their particular place in the body.

Here is what I believe the Bible reveals to us. Those called to equipping ministries will need more equipping, mentoring and training. This is an awesome task and must be pursued. Jesus directly trained the initial apostles for at least three years. Paul was already a PhD by the standards of the day, but was in the school of the Spirit for three years before returning to the apostles for a release to further ministry. While these examples do not make formal training mandatory they do speak of a willingness to be trained. The major issue for our day is that this training must be in and of the Spirit of God. If one goes to a Bible training school, it would be best to attend a program that requires the student to seek the Lord with passion and hunger, looking to the Lord for direction. Some may need more time in mentoring than others and all need spiritual fathers for life!

What is my point? Do not scorn training for ministry, neither require a set pattern for it. God's requirements for one will not be the requirement for all. The Lord meets true hunger as we seek Him. The Bread of Life and the New Wine of the Spirit satisfy us. A man or woman, a vessel of the Lord set for that purpose, may deliver these.

I love listening to some believers who decry "official training". They speak of how it is simply not needed and that the Holy Spirit is our teacher and then they tune in to TBN or some other network to *learn from men*, the very thing that they are complaining of. They forget that God meets our hunger with His word, which was *penned by men* at the urging of the Spirit. They are quick to run to prophets, forgetting that the prophet is a servant of the Lord and is a *human being!* In other words, *people* are training them. Yes these are hopefully people filled with God and hungry for the Lord themselves, but people nonetheless.

How is hunger met? We are satisfied when we are engaged in the meal set before us! God is here, by His Spirit, to feed those who are hungry for more of Him. The Lord has set servants in our midst who are equipped and filled with God to train us up in the things of the Lord. They are examples that we can follow as they follow Christ. As we seek the Lord He will be found by us. The key to having our hunger met is to seek the Lord, love His word, invite His presence in worship and prayer, submit to anointed instruction, and eat, my friend, eat! Hungry vessels are most likely to become radical ones. A sure sign of our devotion is a desire for more of the Lord. Hungry? Let the Lord fill you with His Bread and His wine. He has prepared a table before us in the very presence of our enemy! God loves hungry vessels!

Part 3

Being Vessels

CHAPTER 15

The "In-between Place"

In my Bible it is on page 844. In yours it is likely a different page. It is a full blank page. There are no words written on it and yet it speaks loudly of something of the most vital importance. This large white space, that I will call "the in-between place", is so intriguing to me. At first glance it would seem that there is nothing on the page and that it is just a "filler" or separation page.

At first it came to my attention as I was in prayer time. I was drawn to the purity of the page itself. Please indulge me, if you would. It was purely white and seemingly empty of words. Yet I was led of the Spirit to meditate on this page! I wanted to argue with Him about it. "Lord, you know that there is nothing on this page 844 and it seems like a waste of time when there is so much in the Bible that I need to be reading. Why do you want me to spend this important time on such an unimportant page?" His reply began to cause my spirit to sink in remorse for my apparent audacity, daring to even think a thought that would be contrary to what the Holy Spirit was truly pointing out to me. After a few minutes of "nothing" I cried out, "But there is nothing there!" The Lord in His loving-kindness spoke softly to me, "But there is...consider it now."

I know that you must think it strange that a fairly well educated man, one who has walked in the things of God for nearly thirty years would get so hung up on a blank page in the Bible. I appreciate your grace to me right now as I share with you what was revealed to me. You see, the page I am referring to separates the Old from the New Testaments. It is not that I have "run out" of things in the Word to study, it is just that I was "drawn" to ponder the years of supposed "silence" that this page represents. To my amazement I was gently but firmly rebuked by the Spirit for thinking that these 400 years were "nothing years", when in fact nothing could be further from the truth!

It was not a very quiet time at all!

History reveals that the years between the time of Nehemiah and the birth of Christ were not quiet times in the least. In what is called the "inter-testament" period we see that following: the Babylonian exile of the Jewish people and Alexander the Great acquired what is known as the Holy Land. This Greek domination threatened the very existence of Israel as a people. Culturally the Greek language began to take over all languages. Over the many years that followed there were rival governments trying to take over the known world. Egypt, Syria and Greece pre-dominated this period of history and the Roman Empire began in the latter part of this time frame (approximately 63 B.C.). One very evil Greek ruler by the name of Antiochus IV Epiphanes brought a near annihilation of the Jews. He attempted to destroy all copies of the Jewish Torah (the Pentateuch) and required offerings to Greek gods. During the rule of Antiochus IV a revolt by a Jewish family, the Maccabees, brought about the independence of Judah until the Romans took control. In the decades to follow the Messiah was born in Bethlehem, Judea, a region under the control of Caesar Augustus and the vast Roman Empire.

So, where was God during these years and what was He saying?

Here is where my prayer time led me. You see there are "God breathed" seasons of preparation. It is as though the Lord inhales just before breathing out a major wind of revival. It is historic fact to note these "seasons". The real question is, "What was the remnant of God's people doing during these so called "silent" years?"

The answer: *they were doing what the remnant does!* They were being faithful, prayerful, and constantly seeking God. They were looking for the Messiah to come! They were busy doing something vital. <u>It was during this period</u> that the rabbinical leaders, teachers and scholars of the very Word of God, began to assimilate the Scriptures in the known languages of the day. They did this to preserve the record, continue the faith and to prepare the people for their coming revival! It was in these years that the Septuagint (the Greek language translation of the Old Testament) was penned. This gave the Word of God to the people. A vast number of those inhabiting Judea were "Greek speakers". The common language of the ordinary people, like the disciples, was Koine Greek, or the language of the fish market. You see, during these four hundred years God was not silent at all! In fact, He was working through faithful people to do His will. While they had no prophetic voice present in those years and there was no distinguishable revelatory gift in operation, God was directing His remnant to a work that would preserve for us all a lasting testimony. Because it was the language of the people, the known Bible was being published and the way for the Messiah was being set in order! John the Baptist, a somewhat extraordinary man, would prophetically prepare the way for the revelation of the Messiah, Y'eshua (Jesus).

What does this speak to us today?

Many of us have just come through a rather lengthy and powerful "season" in the Lord. God in His sovereignty poured out of His Spirit in ways that many of us had not witnessed before. While there is certainly a question as to whether this time period could be called revival or not, it was evident that God has done a great thing in the earth. Here at Praise! Fellowship, as in many places around the globe, we were blessed in this visitation. God has touched many people in very apparent ways. Many were filled, healed, touched and otherwise restored. In fact it must be testified that God continues to do a work in many lives today. We are still in the afterglow of this time that has been called "the renewal".

At the same time there are many of us who are crying out to

God with a sense of desperation for the "next" of God. For some it feels as though we are trying to "hang on" to what we have known, almost in the way that a friend holds on to another who is about to fall from a cliff! I too get concerned that things do not have quite the same "fire" as they once seemed to have had. I have spoken to other leaders who have been experiencing the same things. I wanted to gain some insight. Is there something slipping away? If that is true what must we do? Is it really something that we do at all? Is there sin? Is there a lacking of some kind? All of these are very legitimate questions that must be asked and answered.

Again, do not get extreme here! God is still saving, healing and filling folks right now. HE is continuing to draw many people to "check out" the things that He is doing.

So why is it that many of us sense a need to examine this so closely? Why is it that so many "renewal churches" are experiencing this same thing right now? Here is what I believe the Lord is revealing in this season:

1. God is not far away from us! He is, by the testimony of His Word, close at hand. He has promised to be with us as we worship Him and He is faithful to His Word!
2. There is more! We have not arrived at some destination. We are still on a path that we must be on. It is vital that we are committed to staying on course!
3. We are called to self-examination, always! We must realize our call to be His vessels in every way. Being available to His work and way is most important. If there is sin, repent. If there is laziness, get with it. If there is correction to be dealt, receive it. But stay on course!
4. There is work to be done. Just as the people of the "in-between" were called to be faithful to a work in the period between the testaments, we are called to be faithful and diligent in this season.
5. This is a revival on the way! God has promised it in His Word! He is faithful. We are called to be a part of what God is doing in the earth.
6. Avoid judging others…there is no excuse for it! There are

some great new books out there that God has given others to write on this issue. Another's place in all of this is not of the importance that looking at ourselves in light of the Word of God is.
7. Remain faithful. I sense in the Spirit that God is giving us an opportunity to get some things corrected in ourselves. He is looking for our obedience and faithfulness. Commitment is merely a "word" unless it is accompanied by our actions. If we need to repent for not praying, tithing, or otherwise missing the mark with the Lord, let us do it and do it now!

There is a great awakening that is about to happen. It will not be easy on the flesh…that is a good thing. God is preparing a bride for Jesus and we are becoming vessels for His purposes in the earth. Let us go after it with all of our hearts!

Do not fear should you think that it is gloom that you see, for the season of the winter's rest is upon the earth right now. Just as it is here in the northern hemisphere at this time, so it is in the Spirit. The winter is a good thing. It allows the soil to rest and prepare for the coming season of growing. Without a rest the soil cannot produce effectively. In the spiritual realm we are looking for a produce that comes from the Creator.

In the past quarter century there have been many attempts to artificially produce things that the earth grows naturally. The results have been interesting. While the fruit of these new bio-techniques has looked pleasant and been larger than normal, the taste has been flat and not as desirable as the "real thing". The Spirit has revealed that when we attempt to have a growth season (revival) in the church by any means other than that which the Lord births in His due season it will be artificial. While it may look good and appear to be larger than normal, it will not be the real thing. We are looking for the real deal and *that* requires waiting on the Lord for His season. We must wait with all diligence and then see the growing season. Remember, that when we come to this growing season it will lead to a great harvest!

The "in-between" place is one that is preparatory for the revelation of God's purposes. Let us see the examples that have gone before us and covenant with God and each other to see it through! I am learning, with much godly struggle, to enjoy the "in-between", because I know that it does not last all that long and when I am diligent and desperate for more of God He will come with His impartation and together we will launch into the new season of fruitfulness in Christ!

One definitive aspect of becoming a *radical vessel* is that you will care about all of this. It will never be good enough to simply settle into a passive mode. Our *waiting* will never be the same as one sitting along the sidelines as life goes by. Our hearts will never be satisfied with anything less than the pursuit of God. So even in the "in-between" place we will be on a mission. That mission is what makes us radical. That mission is our passionate and most holy pursuit. We will not be happy, truly happy, unless and until we are consumed by a fire that is kindled by God, the most radical One. His passion for us is so far above ours for Him. In the season of waiting we are proactively moving on. We are studying the Word for the life and strength that it brings to us. We are praying like never before. We are fasting to gain clarity in our spirit. We are moving when all else seems to be at a standstill. Becoming a *radical vessel* consumes our every waking moment. We go to sleep at night with Jesus on our hearts above and beyond how He was there last night. We have not become extreme in the sense of foolishness, but we have become extremely foolish for the sake of the Gospel of Christ. To the world we look like a fire out of control, but to the Lord we are simply a flame fanned by the passion of the wait. We look for His coming, but not just His eventual and inevitable return to reign. No, we are seeking to have His reign in our lives today!

There are words that do not have a place in the vocabulary of the radical vessel. We do not give up to the temptation to quit, for quitting is not a part of the radical life that we have embraced. We do not even consider the possibility of backsliding for we do not understand that concept. There is no retreat, no bending to other gods, no death which becomes us other than self-denial. As much as our *wait* seems to extend we are fully consumed by the fact that when it does end we will have a glory that does not fade away. Jesus has given this level of passion to us. We are *radical vessels*.

But there is one thing that *radical vessels* have in common. We are "go people". Let us look at the next step in being this kind of vessel.

CHAPTER 16

The "Go Group"

"And He said to them, 'Go into all the world and preach the gospel to all creation.'" Mark 16:15

There is a stirring that is caused by stepping out of our comfort zone. When we step out of the comfort of our home, community, friends and family, for just a season and take the Word to the world something absolutely amazing happens in us. Radical vessels cannot stand to ignore the Great Commission. We do not just go out of obedience to the scriptures although this should be a good enough reason to go. Radical believers are so touched by this verse that we cannot look the other way. We are not able to just sit and listen to others give a testimony of their recent weeklong trip to Mexico or Africa. No, their stories really work in our hearts. We can hardly stay in our seats. We are compelled to break out of our current environment and see God move anywhere and everywhere.

There is a major difference between those I speak of and the high level passion of those who receive a call to permanent and long-term missions fields. I am really speaking to what I call the "Go Group". This group of vessels get stirred with every opportunity to go here and there, wherever God would lead, for a week or so here or a week or so there, just to witness the Lord move among others.

Let me make a bold statement here. *If you really want to get a fire started in your heart and life, sign up for the very next available short-term missions trip that your church is taking to a third world nation!* Go and get your passport! I have challenged our church with this statement: if you will go and get your passport you will be saying to the Lord that you are at least willing to go should he summon. You are indicating a "yes" in your spirit.

Please do not misunderstand, I know that some will never set foot outside their own hometown, let alone the states or Canada. That does not mean that those who do not go on a short-term trip are not in the Father's will. Far be it from me to judge anyone and their walk with God. But consider this: it is the heart of a vessel belonging to the Lord that says "I will" whenever the Spirit moves and confirms something, whether that be going to Mexico or on an relief or rebuilding mission or even taking the Word to the streets in your hometown. The issue is being able to finally come to the place of, "Here am I, send me" (see Isaiah 6:8).

Radical vessels are those people who have stopped listening to the critics who spend their time complaining about the fact that no one is doing anything for the sake of the Gospel but do nothing themselves but rather take seriously their role in the work of the kingdom of God.

Are you passionate about the Lord's presence? Are you ready for more of the Lord? Are you prepared to submit your will to His and get on with it? If you are, you are likely ready for a journey of major consequence, for your life and for the sake of Jesus. If you have decided that being a part of the "go group" is more important than the other things in the back of your mind, like a new car or 4-wheeler or some other toy, then you are getting closer to your real home!

Later I want to explore the things that hold us back and the things that will release us into the fresh, powerful and brand new thing that God wants to do in you today. It is one thing to get the Bible lesson and quite another to move it from the head to the heart and then outwardly to how the Lord would use it and use you. Do not forget that you can have faith to move mountains, but if you do not do something with it, faith just sits there waiting to be exercised (see James 2:20-26). I also want to take a look at how we stay in the vein of what the Lord is doing in this radical hour. I have met far too many people who once burned brightly but today are dimmer than a headlight with a broken alternator. Where did they go? What are they doing now? How can we get them to the place of restoration so God can again burn within their hearts?

To be a part of the "go group" one must consider where he now stands. It is far too easy to simply run around doing things and think that this is the answer to the call. Having a right relationship with Jesus and His church is a vital part of being effective in the mission. There are a few responsibilities that come with the walk. If we are people of God's order we will be more than willing to walk this thing out the way that He has established it. Just as we are seeing a great level of frustration in the larger body of Christ due to disorder and the failure of following God's prescription for His church, the individual has to be in proper submission to the way the Lord does things in order to be effective.

In many instances the larger body of Christ has moved from following a biblical normative to doing things the way we see best. Simply stated in much of the organized or institutional church we have rejected God's blueprint and design for the church and established our own. We assemble councils and committees to set the guidelines disregarding the pattern set forth in scripture and then stand amazed that our way is not working. It has always be puzzling to me that we debate the "politics" of the church at annual conventions and then pass rules, regulations and policies that are so far removed from the Bible that we do not begin to reflect the life of the church as it was originally designed. When it fails we struggle with where we went wrong. I suggest that it is time for a major revolution in church organization. God has not cast aside His church! Jesus is returning for a bride that is called "the church". Those who have removed themselves, corporately or individually from God's way are going to be held accountable for their actions or lack thereof.

In First Corinthians 5 we see the church dysfunctional. In fact this whole letter deals with the need for the church to find God's order! In this particular instance the wayward member has not been addressed in the way of righteousness. Before looking at the "brother", as he is called in the Word, let us look at the church itself. Paul must address the church not the sinner, because the actions of the church are a more significant blight. Their unwillingness to address the situation, whether out of fear or laziness, brings grief not only to their apostle but also to the Lord God Himself. Why? Because God's order has been ignored. Not one leader among them has taken the steps that will both correct the brother and bring peace and a good testimony to the church at Corinth. If they had done so this issue would not be presented for our understanding in the scriptures.

How does this apply to the issues of the "go group"? If a person has reached the point of candidacy for the office of radical they must understand that there is a relationship with the church that must be followed. As I address this issue there will be some who say that this is simply the ramblings of a pastor trying to preserve the role of pastoral authority...they will see it as self-serving. If that be the case, I suggest that those thinking such things are already prone to rebellion rather that revolution. You see, God has not changed His mind about how things have been established by Him!

God's order for those who serve

Paul and Barnabas were, at the time, two candidates for the office of "radical vessel". We do not know too much about Barnabas, but we do have some insights about Paul. Acts 9 reveals the way in which the future apostle was called to salvation and ministry. Interesting to note is that we really do not see Saul as one who was seeking a relationship with God through Jesus. He was zealously carrying out his "ministry" on behalf of the Jewish leaders of his day. He was going after the Messiah followers. Jesus shows up and changes everything.

Following his conversion to Christ, Saul hangs out with the disciples in Damascus, Jerusalem and other places. He then disappears for a few chapters. By later testimony Paul was attending the School of the Spirit in the wilderness. He reappears with Barnabas at an elder's meeting in chapter 13. There, the prophets and teachers are fasting and seeking the Lord for guidance. The Holy Spirit speaks loudly and clearly that He is sanctifying the two for a powerful ministry, they are then sent out by the leaders to this mission.

"So after they had fasted and prayed, they placed their hands on them and sent them off." Acts 13:3 NIV

I believe that this passage, along with many others, affirms that there is a *God-order* for things in the church; that we are called to follow it; and that God's blessing of lasting fruitfulness is the result. Let me expand upon this:

The "go group" is comprised of people who have decided to do several things.

1. They have made themselves available to God.
2. They have spent time in the School of the Spirit, whatever that may mean. One thing is certain: it will take some time to do! The first disciples spent three years with Jesus Himself. Paul spent three years in the wilderness school. Moses spent 40! The "go group" understands that, although excited and willing to go NOW, they will be required of the Lord to spend some major time of preparation.
3. They are properly submitted to leadership in the body of Christ, those who have already paid the price and are walking in proper order.
4. They are people committed to prayer and fasting in order to seek the face of God and are unwilling to go unless the presence of the Lord goes also (see Exodus 33:15).
5. Upon being sent, they will continue to walk in proper relationship with the body of Christ and be a part of a local gathering, pastor and other leaders. They will be "sent" forth from the body they relate to. They will be accountable to the Lord and to the church sending them.

Recently some of the church experienced yet another failure by a man who was thought by some to be a leading voice in the prophetic movement. I say "some of the church" because many would not even recognize the man's name, while others placed him on such a pedestal that they are likely going through some degree of turbulence over it today. This man authored many books, spoke at many conferences and was generally thought of as a general in the move of God. Other major leaders around him required nothing of him regarding submission or proper biblical order because, by their own admission, they thought of the man as being above and beyond the need for pastoral or local church overseeing. They were wrong and today they admit it plainly. Unfortunately, for some the repentance of the leaders may be too little, too late. For most it will work out. For the one who has failed there is still a long way to go. But the real issue that I want to point up is our need to never excuse anyone from God's pattern for doing things. He has an order and when we get outside of that order, no matter who we are, we are asking for trouble.

In Leviticus 16 God gives Moses instructions to be delivered to Aaron as he enters the ministry of the office of high priest. One of the most striking parts of this scripture is where God says, "Tell your brother Aaron not to come whenever he chooses into the Most Holy Place..." (16:2). In chapter ten Aaron witnesses the death of two of his sons at the hand of God. What was their crime? They chose to not follow God's order! Their spiritual additive of incense produced unauthorized fire and the fire of God came down and consumed them rather than the sacrifice on the altar (10:1-2). The Lord wanted Aaron to understand that the priestly office required some things of him. He had to do it God's way or die!

We are in an age in the church where people seem to be choosing their own way of doing things. They are passionate about the Bible but seem to have no concept of submitting to God or His authority. They have not "fathers" and therefore are lone rangers in their walk. This will produce unauthorized fire and God will not be pleased. Likewise, however, those to whom authority to oversee has been given must also take very seriously the need to be submitted to others with their walk. We seem to be in an age filled with titles and offices but not much relationship. The New Testament speaks more of offices than titles. We would do well to pay careful attention to God's order. I think that if the "go group" of radical vessels will stay in relationship with their pastors and local assembly they will find a greater level of peace and fruitfulness.

The cry of the heart of those who answer the call to go to the lost will be met with an anointing for service when a decision has been made to follow God's blueprint for the church. Always remember that "radical" does not mean "rebellious". Also remember that there is no perfect church gathering. Leaders are not perfect. They will not always get it right. But this fact alone does not permit us to subrogate the need to be in proper relationship with God's order.

"Consequently, he who rebels against the authority is rebelling against what God has instituted, and those who do so will bring judgment on themselves." Romans 13:2 NIV

God desires to have the "go group". He is looking for willing vessels that will take seriously the call to the world around us. The harvest is plentiful and the workers are few.

CHAPTER 17

Getting There From Here

There is no question that we are nearing the "end of the age". Of course I have no idea of what all of that means. But there is no doubt that the signs of the times would indicate that the need in the earth for the gospel is great and that we are being called to go after the harvest, shepherd the flock and otherwise become more effective in our call today.

Recently I was in the Philippines taking part in a conference of believers at a significant church. In speaking with the missionary pastor it was disclosed that the beginnings of that church a number of years ago was the result of major street evangelism. However, there had been a remarkable change over the past year or so. While reaching the lost was still the priority of the church they had discovered that the current need was to more effectively pastor the flock that was now well established. Simply put, they needed to teach and care for the flock that was now coming to some level of maturity. It could no longer be simply or strictly a matter of evangelism, the church needed care. There are many wounded that land on the doorway of the church and need restoration before finding their destiny in Christ. Once healed these will make the most radical of vessels in our midst.

I am again reminded that the Bible speaks of apostles, prophets, evangelists, pastors and teachers. The church cannot be whole unless all of these ministries are functional. Radical vessels need to understand this. The Holy Spirit is restoring this list of offices in our day!

We need to grasp the call to evangelize and expand the kingdom while at the same time see the need to establish it. We seem to have the pendulum swinging to one extreme or another. As a pastor/teacher I will likely have a myopic view of ministry from the perspective of a shepherd. An evangelist may only see the need to save the lost. A prophet may be totally focused on a fresh revelation of Jesus to His people. As radical vessels we must come to see the whole picture and respect (a word that the church has yet to embrace) each office holder and each member as a vital part of the move of God. The next major move of the Lord, I am convinced, will not be myopic in the least, but will see the whole body as functional and needed.

So how do we move from where we are today to where we can be? How do we take the energy that is created by radical vessels and constructively move toward the goal?

"I press on toward the goal for the prize of the upward call of God in Christ Jesus." Philippians 3:14

The radical vessel understands that maturity is a process and that we need to aim for this type of growth in our lives before the Lord. We also know that we are given a life to live in this earth and that there is joy in the journey. Far too many who have felt the burning of God inside have gone to a place of *unauthorized fire*. This has come in very sincere times for most. We are filled with the Spirit, passionate about worship and on fire for God. When we encounter those who have not yet come into this journey we are at times perplexed. We then can easily fall prey to the notion that we are alone in this and begin to isolate ourselves from others.

We can move to a place of feeling a sense of spiritual superiority and start judging others and their walk. If we do not catch this early on we are prone to go somewhere that we will likely regret later on. A true radical for God understands that there is a dynamic that only comes when we walk with the larger body of Christ. True humility marks our path and we are only satisfied when we are learning and leaning. Learning comes from the Word and the impartation of that teaching through others appointed and anointed by God toward us. Leaning is what we do in relationships. We lean first into the Lord and then into His church, an imperfect gathering of people who are together finding the Lord daily. There is an individual component and a corporate membership. We are not complete vessels until we understand this and choose to walk in it. We will need to trust and respect others. This will create in us a vulnerability that is a bit scary for sure. But if we first put our trust in God we will be able to lean into others around us in the journey. We need each other!

One thing to look for in your own life is the exclusionary symptom. This manifestation is when you begin to feel like you are the only one who is doing anything for the kingdom! You are the only one witnessing, praying, walking with Jesus...the Elijah syndrome, "I alone am left." (See 1 Kings 19:10).

Avoiding the Elijah Syndrome

Truth is that most do not want to have a superiority complex. What must we do to avoid this tragedy in our lives?

Humble yourself in the sight of the Lord that He may raise you up for His purposes alone. This is really not about you! It is about the King of glory.

When you begin to hear yourself developing a critical spirit toward the church, remember that you are a part of the church. Give yourself to wholesome talk about others and, please hear my heart, grow up! You are acting immaturely and you really do not have to. You need the church and they need you. To become a radical vessel you will go through seasons of testing and trial. One of the great tests of your walk is found in your correction of this matter in your life.

Getting there

Getting "there" from "here" will not always be easy. There will be bumps along the way. We will fail and see others fail too. But maturity says that this is a part of the path to which we are all called. God will not leave nor forsake us. He will always be present with us. He has ordained all Christians, not just a few select ones, to be radical vessels. He will assign us to a life that calls us away from worldliness but not out of the world altogether. He beckons us to come to Him always…in good times and bad…so that He may tend to our deepest need.

I so want to be a radical vessel. My heart is to go the distance and to finish well. I have grown to love Jesus more each day and to love His body the church more everyday as well. I do not want to rebel but need to be revolutionary. There is much to gain and a great price to pay if I am going to be this kind of vessel. If I stay with the plan and proceed with the journey God will make a provision that will cause me to be honorable, revived, pure, prepared, restored, in His favor, knowing His presence, a man with a purpose, completely furnished in Christ, and hungry for more! While there may be times of the "in-between", where I am not really hearing much or even seeing much, I will know that this journey requires dedication to a result yet unseen. I long to be ready to go when He says "go" and have the promise that as long as my eyes are fixed on Jesus, He will guide and lead me to the place where ultimately I will see Him face to face! I am becoming a radical vessel. Will you dare yourself to dance this dance, to sing this song and to put yourself on the Potter's wheel that you will be formed for His call to you as a *Radical Vessel*?

"Let us fix our eyes on Jesus, the author and perfecter of our faith, who for the joy set before him endured the cross, scorning its shame, and sat down at the right hand of the throne of God. Consider him who endured such opposition from sinful men, so that you will not grow weary and lose heart." Hebrews 12:2,3 NIV

CHAPTER 18

Some 21st Century Radical Vessels

"I have come to cast fire upon the earth; and how I wish it were already kindled!" - Jesus in Luke 12:49

Without a doubt I could name several ambassadors of Jesus that are well known as true pioneers of faith today. These are regarded by many as truly *radical vessels*. Some of them are mentioned or quoted in this book. However, it is not those that I wish to write about at the conclusion of this work. Instead, I wish to mention a few men and women of God that you will not likely recognize. These are faithfully ministering around the globe and are some of the most radical people I know.

The following servants are so tuned in to the Spirit of God that I am envious to possess what they have. They are truly servants of God. I will address three specific areas with each one: 1) some biographic information will introduce them to you; 2) their current work is vital to understanding why they would be called "radical vessels", and 3) how they are impacting the world around them will challenge us to be likewise on fire.

I mention these people to give you some examples of those who do not seek glory for themselves but choose to exalt the Lord alone. In fact, they would be reluctant to be mentioned at all. However, we need to have their model to follow and therefore I humbly present them to you.

Rev. Marian Hartley

Marian is a dear friend of ours and comes from our fellowship. Raised in the small community of Russell, Pennsylvania, Marian grew up working at her father's greenhouse. Her family was not comprised of many believers in Christ, but at the right time God saved this woman through Jesus.

Marian's call to ministry began when she was a young girl and always "saw" herself in Alaska. She was trained as a nurse and at one point felt that God was sending her to Alaska to work in hospitals that served the native populations. After working in that field for a season, Marian knew that her real call was to preach and serve the Eskimos of the Arctic regions.

The Assemblies of God credentialed her as a home missionary and she began her work in Sitka and then moved to the small bush village of Shaktoolik on Norton Sound.

Shaktoolik is a community of Inupiat Eskimos consisting of about 250 men, women and children. In the village are a school, two churches, a general store and small power plant and is a checkpoint village for the Iditarod. The Inupiat Assembly meets in a small building connected to the parsonage. The other church is an Evangelical Covenant church. Neither church is well attended, although the village has a long heritage of Christian witness. Like many native communities, addiction and poverty run hard and take a large toll on this village. Teenage suicides are far too common and a sense of hopelessness is pervasive among the people. The Inupiat people are dear ones.

In 2003 Trudy and I had the honor of taking a small team by bush plane into this remote town ninety miles from the Arctic Circle. It was on this mission that we saw firsthand the passionate work of this vessel known as Pastor Marian.

Our friend has been in Shaktoolik for the past five years. In this season Marian has seen some good progress and many times of seeming failure. What makes Marian a radical vessel is simply this: she truly believes that God is at work and that He has a passion for these precious people. She has a vision for the children and teenagers. God has given her a compassion that motivates her and has also set with her a powerful intercessor among the people.

I consider Marian a radical vessel not because she preaches to thousands, but because she preaches to a few with the firm conviction that God has a plan...and He does. While it could not be said that revival has hit this village as yet, it is possible. Pastor Marian believes, as we do, that God is restoring these people. He is redeeming their heritage and bringing hope to them through His Word.

A hundred years ago, well meaning missionaries came to this village to bring the good news. What they found was a people who danced, drummed and otherwise embraced Shamanism. Not knowing exactly what to do, the missionaries convinced the people to give up their practices and worked to remove their language and traditions. I believe that the depression seen in this and other communities like it is a direct result of the white man's complete disregard for the customs and traditions that God could redeem. Marian's vision is that these things must be restored, but to glorify the Lord Jesus Christ. We join with her in this quest.

This pastor survives on the same subsistence living that the native people do. She and the church make it on only a few thousand dollars each year. Shaktoolik is not a "beautiful" part of Alaska by tourist standards, although it possesses a beauty of its own. Every home in this village has received the witness of the gospel of Jesus. Not all have responded. Out of shear obedience to God this radical vessel is at work. She brings the light of the Lord in a place experiencing only an hour of daylight in mid-winter and only a few hours of rest in summer's twilight. This and countless other Eskimo villages will receive the Word and many will be saved because there are radical vessels like Pastor Marian bringing light into darkness.

Pastor Don Richter

It is most likely that you have never heard of this man. However, Don is a spiritual father to many including me. Most of his "sons", however, are in remote and far off places in the earth.

By training and trade Don Richter was a businessman and a rather successful one. When Jesus saved him Don came to understand that he was called to serve the Lord. After serving as the founding pastor of a thriving church in the Mid-Hudson valley, Don and his wife Lois continued their incredible journey with Harvest Preparation International Ministries, a work that they had started while pastoring.

The vision of Harvest Prep is to provide training and relationship to third-world leaders in the church. Taking teams of mature pastors and leaders to some of the most difficult areas of the world, training is provided to pastors and other leaders where formal preparation is not readily available. Literally thousands of lives have been shaped and strengthened through this ministry in such places as Cuba, southern and central Mexico and Africa.

Pastor Don, as he is affectionately known in these locations, is one of the most on-fire men I know. He is a humble visionary who surrounds himself with others of like calling, taking the risks associated with this kind of ministry.

What makes Don Richter a "radical vessel"? He has a "yes" in his spirit, a wisdom that comes from God alone and is not afraid to tackle what others consider to be impossible. He is able, by the grace of God, to put together apostolic teams that are humble, sensitive and prophetic. These teams, raising their own financial support, give of their time and fire to bring life to the church in hard places in the earth.

Pastor Don's success will not be measured in this life particularly, but rather in the coming kingdom, when it will be discovered that many thousands of churches and villages in the world have be impacted by leaders trained directly or indirectly by HPIM apostolic teams.

Benjamin Mwima

I thought I really knew something about prayer. I actually believed that I was a praying man of God, that is, until I met Ben Mwima.

Brother Benjamin is from Uganda. He met his wife Imelda in a prison camp under the regime of Idi Amin. While a university student Ben and his friends were arrested for boldly witnessing for Christ on the streets. When confronted about their "illegal" activities, Ben admitted what they were doing and implicated his friends as well. None were ashamed of the gospel of Jesus.

While in prison Benjamin's faith and prayer life grew strong. The Holy Spirit gave him step-by-step instructions each day that resulted in salvations in the prison. One of his prison jobs was to mop up the blood from the floors following the tortures and deaths invoked by Amin's efficient work force. At one point Ben and one of his friends were instructed to rape a woman in front of the guards. They refused and instead witnessed to the guards. The woman would become Ben's wife after their release!

Benjamin, Imelda and their children relocated to Kenya after Amin was deposed. Called as an evangelist and teacher, Ben has written several books and travels extensively teaching the issues of a serious prayer life. Ben is a radical vessel for Jesus who is under the constant attack of the enemy. He understands true persecution and encourages the body of Christ to begin asking God for the harder things.

Pastor Joseph Lacavo

Also an African, Pastor Joseph is a rather unique leader of leaders. Preferring to be known only as a pastor, Joseph is the ultimate apostolic leader.

Eldoret, Kenya, in the northwest part of that nation, is a city that God has obviously picked as a centerpiece for prayer and revival for East Africa. Joseph is a very attractive African man, sensitive to the Holy Spirit and humble nearly to a fault.

One of the unique visions that God has given Joseph is the

establishment of Prayer Mountain, just outside of the city. Prayer Mountain is providing a place for contemplative prayer and worship atop a mountain from which one can see not only Kenya but also Uganda on a clear day.

Respected highly by the business community of Eldoret, Joseph Lacavo ministers daily in a meeting for the business leaders. They gather to hear the word of God during their lunch break each day, coming from many different church backgrounds. Many churches have been established through his ministry and he is a true spiritual father to the men who lead these churches.

Why is this man considered to be a radical vessel...Rev. Joseph Lacavo has a vision to reach all of East Africa in his lifetime and he is doing something about it! The poverty of Eldoret will not keep this anointed servant from the assignment God has given him.

Bob Sorge

Many will recognize this name. Bob Sorge is regarded by many to be one of the most prolific authors on the issues of worship in our time. His book *Exploring Worship* is considered to be a classic on worship ministry and has been translated into many languages. He has written nearly a dozen books and travels the globe as a teacher to the body of Christ at large.

Bob served as a Bible college instructor and was a pastor for many years. His book *In His Face* outlines the beginnings of sorrows that this servant has been experiencing for several years now. In short, a serious vocal injury sustained during surgery left Bob literally without a voice. But what the enemy intended for evil the Lord has permitted for His glory.

While Bob Sorge awaits his physical healing, he teaches the body of Christ the vital message of the crucible of God's fire and passion. Simply stated, Bob is a man of prayer.

I have had the privilege of traveling with Bob in ministry a number of times and count him as one of my closest friends. A number of years ago I accompanied him on a trip to Europe and Russia. It was there that I discovered the despicable condition of my own prayer life.

Because Bob has very little voice to work with he spends much of his time on his face before the Lord. When one first encounters this in my brother it is a bit disarming and unsettling. As I found myself wanting to "tour" the cities where we were ministering, Bob found his greatest times in hotel rooms on his face before the Lord. His motive? My interpretation is this: my friend simply and profoundly wants communion with God!

His message may be a bit hard to take for some who believe that the Christian life is nothing but victory atop of victory. But the fact remains that this man of God is a radical vessel imparting a thirst for intimacy with the Lord. He advocates for wholehearted worship before God and teaches others to pursue this with a passion.

When with him I am challenged in my life. When reading his books I am changed in my perspective and walk. I find myself wanting more and more of God. You see, radical vessels make us want what they are getting!

Ronnie Harjo

I cannot complete this chapter or this book without recognizing a radical vessel among the people of the First Nations. While I am not aware of one drop of Native American blood in me, God has birthed a cry in my spirit for the people most often forgotten and profoundly persecuted among us.

Apostle Ronnie Harjo is exactly that...an apostle of Christ. I do not regard him in this way to elevate him but to recognize the work that God is accomplishing in and through him.

Again, most will not recognize this man by name. Ronnie is a Seminole Indian from Oklahoma. Like Benjamin Mwima in Africa, Ronnie is an apostle of prayer for his people in America. His life before he knew Christ was wild and crazy. His walk with Jesus is radical to say the least.

A quiet and contemplative man of God, Ronnie and his Hawaiian wife Valerie, carry a burden for the Native people to come to Christ. He meets regularly with Indian nation leaders, not yet believers in Christ, to offer support and prayer for them. He preaches whenever possible to those on the reserves of America, in

Oklahoma and the Dakotas and spends large blocks of time in prayer and fasting at a little house in upstate New York, known as Anna's House of Prayer.

Ronnie has traveled to Israel and Cuba as a part of delegations to the nations. He is often in the company of other recognized First Nation leaders like Dr. Jay Swallow and Nigel Big Pond. While this humble man may not consider himself to be one, he is truly a radical vessel with compassion for all people, especially those who were the first people on the American continent before it was called America.

A few years ago Trudy and I, and a delegation from our fellowship, had the privilege of being with Dr. Swallow, Ronnie and other Native Christian leaders on a special ministry expedition to Plymouth Rock. It was there that my eyes were first opened to the beautiful people that Ronnie is a part of. His passion for prayer, the Word and people makes Ronnie Harjo a 21st century radical vessel!

I could name several other radical vessels. Most of them will not be up for any awards or ever be recognized in Christian periodicals. They will not likely receive a Dove Award or Nobel Prize. They are simply servants with one thing on their hearts…knowing God, sharing His hope and goodness and making an indelible impression upon most everyone they encounter.

The good news is that each and every one of us can become a vessel in the service of our Lord and Savior Jesus Christ. The call to get out of the religious box and press on toward the high call of Jesus is to each one of us. We do not have to hold an office or write a book or song. We do not have to preach to millions or be known by others. Every Christian is called to be as radical as Peter and John as they offered all they had to the lame man in Acts 3. Each one of us can function like Paul before Felix or Agrippa. The Holy Spirit will give us what is needed for this call.

How do we come to the place of being known in the courts of Heaven as radical vessels…by getting a "yes" in our hearts and then taking that "yes" to all around us.

You can do it! Yes, *you* can! Let us join together in the holy pursuit of Jesus and of His call upon us to be….*radical vessels*!

Epilogue

I love the church because Jesus loves the church. After all it is His body and He has designed it as a lean, mean fighting machine. We are designed for warfare and it will take truly radical vessels to accomplish what the church is being sent to do.

Yet, there is need for change in the church if we are to become effective. Change is inevitable. God is always shaping and molding the church to be a more formidable force. But change cannot be forced to happen by human hands or manipulation. As much as you may want to see change happen, the best place to bring it about is still on your knees!

I want to issue the church in this day a challenge. Could we decide here and now that this thing belongs to God? Could we make a profound decision to take our hands off what God owns? It might be possible to see the fingerprints of God alone on what happens next, if we simply release it all to the Lord.

To the pastors and spiritual leaders of the church I would suggest that we all prepare for the church to look quite differently from what it does today. For some this is really great news. I know it is for me. I have longed for the new reformation that God promised many years ago. It seems to me that reformation is absolutely necessary on a cyclical basis or we become stagnant and spiritual death enters.

It will, however, be quite a challenge. If you are glued to your pension and job security as a pastor, you might be in for some stark reality. We will be required to participate in the same way that leaders of old did...with great cost. The day of soft ministry, I predict, is nearing an end in North America, Europe and the UK.

To the body of Christ...I warn you...fall in love with Jesus and learn to love what He loves. The church is His body and your commitment to the body is required. There is no longer any excuse for rebellion and foolishness. Love Him – love His church. If you do not you will live your days with great difficulty.

To all: we must understand that God is not looking for rebels, but revolutionaries. He is not seeking wayward warriors, but radical vessels. He really wants us to cooperate with Him and be His vessels in the earth.

The future is bright for the church. We are on our way to perfection! Jesus is coming for a spotless (perfect) bride and He is coming soon. I am convinced that this is the most exciting time for the church since the days of its birth. As we covenant with God and each other we will enter into the newest and greatest phase of our Christian experience...that of the *radical vessel!*

For this and other materials and CDs from Dale or to schedule him to speak:

www.worshipplace.org
mail@worshipplace.org

Restored! Ministries
RD#3 Box 3087
Russell, PA 16345
814-757-4357

This book and other materials are available at your local Christian booksellers.

Printed in the United States
33308LVS00005B/394-549